HOW TO TURN
AN **INTERVIEW**
INTO A **JOB**

SIMON AND SCHUSTER
NEW YORK

WITH APPRECIATION . . .

*To Bev, for better or for worse; and
to Fred, for best or forget it!*

Copyright © 1983 by Jeffrey G. Allen, J.D., C.P.C.
All rights reserved
including the right of reproduction
in whole or in part in any form
Published by Simon and Schuster
A Division of Gulf & Western Corporation
Simon & Schuster Building
Rockefeller Center
1230 Avenue of the Americas
New York, New York 10020

SIMON AND SCHUSTER and colophon are
registered trademarks of
Simon & Schuster
Designed by Irving Perkins Associates
Manufactured in the United States of America

10 9 8 7 6 5 4 3 2 1
10 9 8 7 6 5 4 3 2 1 pbk.

Library of Congress Cataloging in Publication Data
Allen, Jeffrey, date.
    How to turn an interview into a job

    Bibliography: p.
    Includes index.
    1. Employment interviewing.   I. Title.
HF5549.5.I6A44 1983   650.1′4   83-487
ISBN 0-671-47173-2
        0-671-47299-2 Pbk.

by Jeffrey G. Allen,
J.D., C.P.C.

To all those intelligent, talented,
creative, industrious, energetic
people among the underemployed and unemployed:

May these keys unlock your potential.

Contents

CHAPTER IX
The Better Letter: Follow-Up into Follow-Through 78
Writing a follow-up letter and writing one that gets you hired are two different things. If you are using form letters and getting them in reply, you'd better reform. You will learn exactly what to use and how to use it.

CHAPTER X
The Experience Express Card: How to Leave Home with It 83
It's time to cast aside all the myths about experience in our society and adopt a no-nonsense, no-waiting strategy to get it.

CHAPTER XI
Analyzing Advertising: Help with the "Help Wanted" 87
The "help wanted" section looks perfectly straightforward, but it's not—watch out for the curves! Here are five types of ads and what they really mean.

CHAPTER XII
Placement Services: The Job Intelligence Network 91
Most people don't understand the function of placement services. Knowing the three basic types and how to use them is indispensable in switching your career into the fast track. They're the conductors; you're the engineer.

CHAPTER XIII
Looking While You're Still Employed: Isn't Everybody? 96
You're measurably more marketable, secure, and confident while still employed. This is a distinct

advantage in being hired if you understand how
to keep your options open. Now, you'll be shown
how.

Introduction

I've spent my entire career in the job placement field, and it all comes down to this:

1. The interview is almost all that counts.
2. The interview is a highly predictable, controllable event, with only the places and faces changing.

Everything else—research, phone calls, letters, resumes—is simply backup for that crucial meeting.

Interviewing should be considered nothing more than packaging yourself for sale. The only difference between selling yourself and selling something else is that you are both the goods and the salesperson. In this sense, the interviewing process is unique and your success can be really exciting. I realize that you may feel anxious or frustrated right now, but this book will give you the confidence you need, and much more.

A successful interview is deceptively simple: it is the minute, almost imperceptible nuances that make the difference. These are specific, proven techniques—nothing more, nothing less.

Soon, you'll discover that exploring your career world and discovering yourself in the process is more interesting, enlightening, and even more enjoyable than all the psychotherapists' couches, biofeedback mechanisms, and self-help courses you will ever find.

One of the first things I learned in my personnel career was that people don't change, circumstances change. A typical example is the employee who is eased out of one company for poor work performance, then goes to another and becomes a superstar. Out of a bad marriage into a good one; failing at one school and becoming an honor student at another; the has-been actor who wins an Oscar. The opposite also occurs just as often.

Sounds familiar, doesn't it? What is really happening?

Nobody is changing, but different *circumstances* are bringing out different *attributes*. That is why internalizing failure is such an illogical, fallacious thing to do. (Internalizing success is illogical too, but at least it gives you self-confidence.)

Forget it—don't fight it. The face in the mirror will always be essentially the same. It's a lot easier to change your circumstances. Life is too short to be slaving away at some dead-end job or knocking on doors. You'll never really know whether you like a job until several weeks after you find the rest room anyway. Plan carefully, get hired, and if you don't like it, go out and get hired again! You'll probably increase your salary and end up ahead of the game.

Worried about your work history? Summarize or omit parts of it. Worry about your life!

I remember huffing and puffing at some recent college grad like myself, trying to convince him that my new employer should also be his. All the right words were there. He listened patiently, and when I caught my breath, he smiled at me with a knowing grin and said, "One fun factory is no better than another, only different."

That was in 1966, and I've never forgotten the wisdom of that statement. Today, he'd probably break into a chorus of *9 to 5.*

Now, I will finally have the chance to prove my theory

that the best person for the job is usually someone who can get hired. I am convinced that the people who interview successfully are the people who are promoted faster, have more self-esteem, and bounce back from the ravages of corporate life faster and higher than anyone else.

I hope that all the hers and shes in this world will understand that the hims and hes in this book are used only for consistency. Until our society develops a neuter term, that's the best I can do. My thoughts are with you every step of the way.

Now, let's get started!

Resume Roulette: How to Play the Game

Literally hundreds of books and articles have been written about resume preparation. The "help wanted" section of any Sunday newspaper contains advertisements by services offering to prepare resumes designed to unlock the interviewer's door. However, the only jobs generated by most of these were for the writers. There is no way to insure that your resume will even be read, let alone forwarded!

This has led some people to wonder whether your chances of getting hired are actually better *without* a resume. The premise is that "if you never do anything, you'll never make a mistake." If Babe Ruth thought that way, his 1,330 strikeouts would not have occurred. Of course, he would not have hit 714 home runs either. Which are remembered?

To understand why resumes are required, it is necessary to consider the plight of the interviewer. Most interviewers are inundated with a flood of different resumes in a variety of shapes, sizes, and colors. Since resume writing is indeed an art, the old saying "I don't know what's good, I only know what I like" fully applies here. In addition, even the most conscientious interviewer soon learns that insisting on resumes reduces telephone time and awkward explanations to applicants. It is nothing more than his way of maintaining his sanity and his job. When blind box advertisements are used, he can even take a lunch break.

Since there is no standard form for writing a resume, you can understand the fallacy of the words "We have evaluated your background..." in the form rejection letters most resumes generate. However, survival of the interviewers of this world depends on resumes; and for professional, management, administrative, and clerical positions, you'd better have one.

For our purpose, a resume is nothing more than a tool to get your foot in the interviewer's door. (It's not really locked, there's only a chair behind it.) A good one results in an appointment for an interview; a bad one does not. If buildings were constructed like most resumes, King Kong would have destroyed the world.

Interviewers are so subjective and inconsistent in their responses to resumes that I have described their use as "resume roulette." With that understanding, there are a few general rules which will at least allow you to stay in the game long enough to make the Deep Breath Phone Call.

A resume *should*:

1. BE NO MORE THAN ONE PAGE IN LENGTH

This is frustrating, I know. But an ounce of image is worth a pound of performance. You simply must resist the temptation to clutter your resume with detailed information. Instead, use general phrases that will incite the interviewer to positive action—an invitation for an interview.

Use phrases like:

"Developed a series of . . ."
"Organized several . . ."
"Was responsible for a number of . . ."
"Consistently performed . . ."
"Was promoted to progressively responsible positions in . . ."

2. BE AT LEAST TEN-POINT SIZE IF TYPESET, OR TWELVE-PITCH SIZE IF TYPED

You can vary the typefaces, boldness, and underlining for interest, but conservative styles will increase the readability of the resume. My personal preference is Press Roman type if printed, or Courier if typed with a carbon ribbon. These sizes and styles are readable, available, and acceptable.

3. BE PRINTED WITH BLACK INK ON WHITE PAPER

Ivory stock can also be used and the weight should be at least twenty-four pound. Gray would be acceptable, but is often difficult to read and photocopy. Any other ink or paper colors are a mistake. Your relationship with the interviewer is still too fragile, and your resume may receive attention for a negative reason. Save your individualism for your promotion party.

4. HAVE AT LEAST A ONE-INCH BORDER

This is primarily for esthetic reasons, but it is common for interviewers to write comments in the margins. If another sheet is required to do so, many will just move on to the next resume.

5. CONTAIN YOUR NAME, ADDRESS, AND TELEPHONE NUMBER CENTERED AT THE TOP

If you move or change telephone numbers, prepare another resume. When starting at the personnel department, this may also be done by attaching it to an updated application. After all, it's only one page.

6. CONTAIN A FEW CHOICE ITEMS OF PERSONAL DATA

Emphasize credentials and career-related affiliations.

7. SUMMARIZE YOUR EXPERIENCE, WITH THE MOST RECENT EMPLOYER AND POSITION FIRST

Whether you are a generalist or a specialist, this section of your resume can be written in several different ways. You will find that working backwards from the kinds of positions you want will help you to focus on the areas of emphasis. Listing or summarizing similar responsibilities is acceptable, but you must be *concise*. This is known as the "chronological" resume.

Some authorities advise a "functional" resume generalizing your duties when you have changed jobs more frequently than every two years. Interviewers are accustomed to application forms with chronological sequence, and therefore the narrative that a functional resume recites turns them off. Further, it is almost impossible to draft a generalized resume without looking like you're hiding the truth. Use a chronological approach, but combine and omit short-term employment. There is no reason for you to include everything at this stage of the game.

A resume *should not*:

1. UPDATE OR EMPHASIZE EXPERIENCE IN HANDWRITING

As we discussed with regard to contact information, updating should only be done through another resume or an attached application neatly typed in advance. Underlining or other emphasizing should either be done at the time the resume is prepared, or not at all. Since the resume is *you* at this point, make sure it has class.

2. CONTAIN INFORMATION ON REFERENCES

Instead, you should state the following: "Personal and professional references are available. They will be furnished

upon request, once mutual interest has been established."
References are too precious to annoy, and you want to be
able to contact them *first*. This rule may be broken if you are
relying on a highly motivated internal referral.

3. STATE A SALARY

This includes the amount you received in former positions
and that which is your requirement. At the early stages, it is
a no-win gamble: it invariably will be too high or too low.
Besides, your value to someone else or even to yourself is irrelevant. This will become more evident when you read
Chapter VII, on salary negotiation.

Moreover, when sent to a *personnel department,* a resume
should not:

1. STATE YOUR OBJECTIVE

This is, unless you know it is the job being offered and you
don't care about being considered for anything else. This is
the problem with introductory letters also. You are just fore-
closing your options. Your objective is getting an *interview!*

2. BE ACCOMPANIED BY A COVER LETTER

This is because a cover letter to an unidentified target can
be counterproductive, pointing you away from the job opening. Unless you *really* know something about the job, or
want to name the source of your referral, resist the temptation. Overworked personnel people will think of it as just
one more piece of paper to shuffle.

However, if you are aiming at a departmental *decision
maker,* an eye-catching cover letter has exactly the opposite effect! It directs you right where you want to be.

A well-written cover letter is crucial in this case: it serves
to introduce you and spark a decision maker's interest. If
you've done your homework, here's a place to use it. Your

letter should meet a prospective employer on his own turf. Start with a comment or two on the company—perhaps concerning recent developments you have read or heard about within the field—and how your work experience might fit in. Close by suggesting your ultimate goal: an interview.

Your homework should include a phone call to the company to find out the correct spelling of the executive's name, his exact title, the full name of the company, and other details. There is no greater turn-off to a prospective employer than having his name or his company's name misspelled.

Like a resume, a cover letter should be neatly typed—not in italic or other "handwriting" typefaces—on white paper (preferably your personal business stationery with your name and address conservatively imprinted).

Your resume will be the goods, but the letter is the package. Therefore, it must reflect quality. We are motivating now, not educating.

The following three items are optional, but worth considering. A resume *may:*

1. CONTAIN A PHOTOGRAPH

Consideration of your face in the hiring process violates federal, state, and local equal employment opportunity laws, except under very limited circumstances. Inclusion of a photograph is therefore a matter of concern to employers, and only a matter of strategy to you. My *personal* opinion is that you shouldn't; my *personnel* opinion is that you shouldn't; but my *legal* opinion is that you can. Whether you should is best left to your judgment. One thing is certain: You're a contestant on "The Gong Show" without an audition. In fact, professional interviewers in some companies will not forward a resume with a photograph attached.

2. CONTAIN INFORMATION THAT RELATES TO SEX, HEIGHT, WEIGHT, HEALTH, MARITAL STATUS, AGE, RACE, RELIGION, PLACE OF BIRTH, OR CITIZENSHIP

As with a photograph, these allow the interviewer or supervisor to decide your fate based upon irrelevant and illegal criteria. You run the risk of a recipient automatically discriminating against you on the basis of this information.

If you want to know the effect of these factors, you can try calling the employer anonymously. Ask a few general questions about its commitment to affirmative action without arousing suspicion. While the information you receive may not be accurate, you will at least have some indication of what to expect. Affirmative action statements in advertisements are meaningless, since they are designed for public and government consumption.

3. USE AN ATTENTION-GETTING GIMMICK

Why not photoreduce and insert your resume into a fortune cookie? An applicant sent me a package like that once. It was a real grabber. I always felt that sending him "No Interest Letter No. 2" was not quite enough. If you happen to see a half-eaten pita bread stuffed with printed paper on some interviewer's desk as you search for a job, this applicant's probably still on the loose.

Your approach should be just to get your foot in the interviewer's door as inconspicuously as possible. Attention? You'll get attention! The rest of you is about to enter. It's time for the Deep Breath Phone Call.

II The Deep Breath Phone Call: "I'll Call You!"

If you have ever waited around for a response to the old "send me a resume" or "submit an application" routine, you need no further convincing that the game just switched from roulette to poker . . . and you'd better know the rules.

Authorities term the internalizing of too many negative responses "rejection shock." This insidious disease has attacked millions, and is now a national epidemic. Heart palpitations when talking with prospective employers is the major symptom, if its victims get that far. But don't worry—here is the cure. Watch out for the side effect: *acceptance shock!*

In his best-selling book *Power! How to Get It, How to Use It*, Michael Korda states: "The person who receives a telephone call is always in an inferior position of power to the person who placed it."[1]

It is this phenomenon, coupled with your anxiety about being hired, that can push your foot out of the interviewer's door while waiting for a call. There is only one way to break the "don't call us, we'll call you" syndrome: *Take a deep breath and call the interviewer!*

I know you will be thinking that the interviewer will be angry at you, and you will therefore not be hired. It's like calling your first blind date. But the reality is that you are just replaying old memories. In fact, the average interviewer who is hiring is so busy trying to place job orders, run advertisements, review resumes, arrange for interviews, interview, verify employment data, check references, rationalize why the position hasn't been filled, and justify exceeding the hiring budget, that there is no *time* to be angry.

As Maxwell Maltz noted in his classic, *Psycho-Cybernetics:*

> A human being always acts and feels and performs in accordance with what he imagines to be true about himself and his environment. This is a basic and fundamental law of mind. It is the way we are built.[2]

The time you call is extremely important, because you want to speak to the interviewer the first time, when he will be most receptive and when you are fully prepared. Statistically, this should be any Tuesday through Friday between 9:00 A.M. and 11:00 A.M.

Mondays are unpredictable and should be avoided, because the interviewer's nervous system will still be stabilizing from the weekend, he might be nursing a hangover (an occupational disease among people who are hiring), new hires are being processed, the employer may be deluged with telephone calls from advertisements in the Sunday paper, and staff meetings are more likely.

Friday mornings are particularly opportune, because employees are terminating, and important decisions are not made on Fridays. This means that the interviewer may learn for the first time that a requisition exists and will defer discussing the position with you by arranging an interview. Friday afternoons are even worse than Monday mornings, because "exit interviews" are generally conducted. These are the "back end" of a personnel position, and the further away you are, the better.

Of course, there are an infinite number of variables in

phone conversations, and you might be calling a supervisor directly. However, the illustration that follows will give you an idea of how to position yourself. The words may vary, but your *attitude* shouldn't.

Now ... sitting comfortably at your desk ... take a deep breath ... exhale slowly ... and place the call:

RECEPTIONIST: Good morning, Company X.

YOU: Hi. Mr. (*last name*), please. This is (*first name*) (*last name*) calling.

RECEPTIONIST: May I tell him what this is regarding?

YOU: (*First name*) asked me for background information regarding the (*title*) position.

RECEPTIONIST: Have you sent us a resume?

YOU: Yes, and I need to fill him in on a couple of points.

RECEPTIONIST: Just a moment, please. I'll ring.... Sorry, the line is busy. Can I take your number?

YOU: No, I'm sorry ... I'll be out of the office. I'd better wait.

RECEPTIONIST: It might be a while.

YOU: I'll wait, thanks.

RECEPTIONIST: I can ring now.

INTERVIEWER: (*First name*) (*last name*).

YOU: Hi, Mr. (*last name*). This is (*first name*) (*last name*). I've been hoping to hear from you to discuss the (*title*) position.

INTERVIEWER: I'm sorry, we've been just deluged with responses. You're still being considered and we hope to let you know within a week or so.

YOU: I know how hectic things must be. I'm under a bit of pressure myself, and it looks like I'll have to make a decision soon. The (*title*) position sounds like a great opportunity, and I'd really like to discuss it personally as soon as possible.

INTERVIEWER: Hang on a minute ... Oh, here's your resume.... When did you leave your last employer?

YOU: I'm sorry, but I'm just about to leave for an appointment. I'd really like to meet you soon. How about tomorrow morning at 8:00?

INTERVIEWER: I can see you at 9:30.

YOU: I'll rearrange my schedule. I'm looking forward to meeting you!

INTERVIEWER: Thank you. See you then.

YOU: Goodbye.

INTERVIEWER: Goodbye.

You have been direct, time-conscious, businesslike, and *affirmative*. You have played out your poker hand in a measured way, and have gathered a few chips. The trick is to get the interviewer on the phone, and you off the phone into his office.

Although I have represented the interviewer as being in the personnel department rather than in the department where you will actually be working, the principles are exactly the same. Generally, the higher the job, the higher the level of the person you can safely contact. The risk is that you will alienate the personnel department, so proceed with caution. Personnel interviewers screen rather than hire. What you don't know can *screen* you, but your ultimate goal is to reach the decision maker!

The rest is easy, because now we're ready for the almighty interview.

How to Schedule Interviews: Timing Is Everything (Almost)

There is a tendency, particularly when you have not been eating regularly, to set up interviews in a random manner. The result is a wide variance in your metabolic rate, attention span, and response time.

If you were laid off or fired from your last job, a measured approach to interview scheduling is the only way to get you emotionally back on the track. It is a psychological fact that physical activity is the best cure for depression. Make interviewing your job until a better one comes along.

The winners in sports and almost every other human endeavor know that consistency is what gives them the edge. You are exercising your interviewing muscles and are jogging . . . not running . . . not walking. If you are out of work, set your goal at one interview around 9:00 A.M. and one interview around 2:00 P.M. Neither should last more than two hours.

Use a calendar with room for daily entries, and set up appointments compulsively: two a day. Soon, you'll have rhythm. It will do wonders for your self-confidence.

As discussed in Chapter II, Friday afternoons are often a

poor time to inquire about your resume, as it is possible that exit interviews are being conducted. However, if you can arrange an interview, this obviously will not be the case.

Another advantage of consistent scheduling is that you will become accustomed to your own reactions when your body chemistry is in the same balance. This will give you an internal predictability and stabilize your nervous system. After a few days, you will find your self-confidence rising.

The two-hour time limit is critical for two reasons:

1. You want it to appear as though you have another commitment. If you don't, make one. People always want what they can't have, and you're starting to run out of gas anyway.
2. It helps you to avoid eating a meal with someone in the hiring process. There is so much that can go wrong in terms of personal mannerisms, offhanded remarks, eating or drinking habits, and etiquette, that the "businessman's special" can be you! For higher-level positions, this may be unavoidable, so attempt to ask discreetly. If it is merely an invitation and not a requirement, graciously decline. You don't want to sacrifice a job for a meal.

IV The Irresistible Interview: Twelve Steps to the Offer

If resume contact is roulette and telephone contact is poker, interview contact is tennis. To the extent that you understand the difference, you will transform interviews into offers.

Interviewing and tennis do not depend upon the chance of roulette or the nerves of poker. Instead, they depend upon approach, practice, and hundreds of conditioned responses. This is why actual experience is so critical to developing your skills at winning, regardless of the court (office) or your opponent (interviewer). You can even make mistakes, as long as there are not too many. Nice to know.

Some novices believe interviewing is a frightening and uncertain mystery. Others are convinced "qualifications" for the "position" are somehow being evaluated. Ask the next person you see, and you will probably get another view. These and other misconceptions arise because the interview is really too complex to be analyzed in its totality.

The development of irresistible interviewing depends upon identifying and controlling twelve chronological steps.

Hang on, Company X, *we're coming through!*

1. FAMILIARIZE YOURSELF WITH THE EMPLOYER.

Developing a profile of each employer you visit not only dramatically increases your ability to impress the interviewer, but is an important first step in reducing your fear of the unknown. Doing your homework in this area can acquaint you with the number of employees, business locations, products, sales, profits, future plans, and a variety of other elements that make up the personality of any business. As you become adept at doing your homework for each employer, you will find that you can take almost 95 percent of the mystery out of interviewing. From the very beginning, your confidence will show.

Our interviewing approach is aimed directly at the *interviewer*, and therefore it really makes no difference whether you are applying for a management position or an entry-level job. Either way, it works!

There are two ways to find out about the employer:

The formal (coward's) way. Your local public library provides a wealth of information on almost all publicly held and many privately held companies. Spending a few hours in the reference section will acquaint you with the correct shelves and buttons on the microfilm machine to find out what you want.

For openers, corporate profiles appear in:

> Annual reports
> *Business Periodicals Index* (H. W. Wilson Company)
> *Dun and Bradstreet's Million Dollar Directory*
> *Moody's News Reports*
> *Moody's Manuals*
> *Standard and Poor's Register of Corporations, Directors and Executives*
> *Standard and Poor's Corporation Records*
> *Thomas Register of American Manufacturers*
> *MacRae's Blue Book*
> *Value Line Investment Surveys*

Since so much information is available, you may be tempted to memorize a lot of statistics about the employer. However, you should *not* do so. Instead, you should merely do your homework by looking the information up, writing down a few items of interest, and moving on to the next employer fortunate enough to have you available for an interview. Review your notes periodically, simply to store the information in your brain. It will be ready for use at the appropriate time without any further conscious thought.

The informal (hero's) way. After the first week of scheduling two interviews a day, you will start to become an "interviewaholic." You may even have received some job offers. If you are still discovering your worth, or if you are an outgoing person anyway, the fastest, most enjoyable, and most effective way to learn about the personality of the employer is by a telephone call. In small organizations, it may be the *only* way, so you should be prepared to do so.

No deep breath required here. Just call the sales department, marketing department, public relations department, or receptionist, and state the purpose of your call. Then plan on doing a lot of listening. You will find that a lot of listening is exactly what you will be doing! People love to talk about their jobs and their companies, and at some point along the line *you* probably will be the one to terminate the conversation.

And here's the bonus: If you play your cards right, you actually may end up with an *internal referral*! There is no more potent entry into any company, since the interviewer will feel obligated to act upon the referral and go forward with an interview. If you look at all good, he'll be inclined to give you the benefit of the doubt. Otherwise, he'll be faced with more than one embarrassing elevator ride if he rejected you for the position.

I'll bet you didn't realize you had friends in such high and low places. Your appreciation should be expressed by a note and return telephone call after the interview. If this seems a little unorthodox, wait until you see the rest of our serves to the interviewer!

2. DRESS PROPERLY.

John Molloy, in his landmark book *Dress for Success*, starts with a premise that over two million people have already bought:

> Those of you who are ... saying that fashion is an art form and not a science are making the same kind of statement as the eighteenth-century doctors who continued to bleed people. I do not contend that fashion is an absolute science, but I know that conscious and unconscious attitudes toward dress can be measured and that this measurement will aid men in making valid judgements about the way they dress.[3]

The reactions to styles, colors, and combinations of clothing are highly predictable. So are the tastes of personnel professionals. Therefore, a carefully chosen interviewing "uniform" on a well-groomed applicant maximizes a favorable response.

The interviewing uniform for men

This is the easiest part, because there is really only one way for any man to dress for almost any employment interview.

Navy blue three-piece suit. Wool and wool blends look better and last longer. Solid colors or subdued stripes are preferred. Gray may be worn, but Brooks Brothers has never been able to manufacture natural-shoulder navy blue suits fast enough to meet the demand. Shiny fabrics should be avoided, and no religious, fraternal, or service pins should be worn.

White long-sleeved dress shirt. Laundered and starched commercially! Your interviewer won't wear a monogram, and therefore, you shouldn't. Collar style should be current, and if French cuffs are worn, cuff links should also not reflect any religious, fraternal, or service affiliation. They should also be the same color as your watch, and neither should be larger than necessary.

Dark blue striped tie. A contrasting color is acceptable, but the predominant color should be the same as your suit. Silk or other thin fabrics are recommended.

Black dress shoes. Almost any style is acceptable, as long as they can be polished well, and are.

Since the uniform for men does not vary for most jobs, you should have at least two or three conservative suits and ties you can use for multiple interviews.

These four items comprise the all-American look in the fashion industry, and it is interesting that almost every consultant agrees on its positive effect. I recently appeared on a radio talk show with a famous designer who commented that when it comes to business wear, "men's fashions" is really a contradiction in terms. There are almost no trends.

The interviewing uniform for women

For some reason, there is far more flexibility in clothing for women. A dress or suit should be worn, preferably in subdued colors and fabrics. The following should be avoided:

V-necks
High hemlines
Jewelry reflecting any religious or organizational affiliation
Gaudy fashion jewelry
Oversized handbags
Excessive make-up
Heavy perfume

There is increasing evidence that extremely attractive women are not hired as readily by men or women. Therefore, if you've got it, don't flaunt it.

If you're budget-minded, the proliferation of discount, wholesale, and factory-direct clothing outlets permits you to acquire an interviewing uniform without taking out a bank loan. Comparison shopping can save you a fortune, and women especially are likely to find famous-maker clothes with different (or no) labels.

Remember, interviewers will look at your clothes, but they won't see the labels.

If you require extensive alterations on ready-to-wear clothes, you might check out custom tailors. The prices are often only slightly higher, but the look is *great!*

For both men and women, regardless of the position, an attaché case is an excellent accessory. They look business-like, and identify you with the interviewer. Dark brown is more popular, but I prefer black for men, since it matches the shoes.

The personnel department is where the game usually begins or ends, and this is where you must score. The case should be wide enough to store a small container of instant coffee (or a few regular tea bags), breath spray, deodorant, cologne, nonsmoking tablets (if necessary), a comb or brush, a gold pen with black ink, a legal pad (the kind lawyers use to intimidate), and six extra copies of your resume. You might also wish to include some information on your background. Borrow the case if you must, but don't use one with somebody else's initials on it.

The exceptions that prove the rule of conservative dress are few and far between: highly creative art and entertainment jobs are where they are found. However, looking the part of the job you hope to find is far less powerful than looking the part of the person who will hire you for it. Yes, you can dress differently. . . if you know what a supervisor in a creative department will be wearing.

Even in fad and fashion industries, personnel professionals tend to be conservative. Their decisions are often made in groups, and to the extent that you vary from middle-class and middle-management values in their structured worlds, success in the interview will vary. You can always dress down a little when you arrive. You can't dress up.

3. ARRIVE ALONE.

You may think that your companion is an asset to bring. You may think that you need moral support. You may think it doesn't matter. You may not even think about it at all. You should.

Nothing good at all can result from bringing someone with you. The prejudices of the interviewer are already a problem, and you will appear to be unprofessional at best. That means the person should make himself scarce and not even appear at the end of the interview.

You and your spouse or companion should also avoid any after-hours social meetings at which your interviewer might be present until you are hired.

We are invoking an absolute rule: HE TRAVELS FASTEST WHO TRAVELS ALONE.

You violate it at your peril.

4. ARRIVE ON TIME.

Any receptionist in America will tell you that appointment punctuality follows a standard bell-shaped curve: one-third of the visitors will be early, one-third will be on time, and one-third will be late. Further, if you are not sensitized to the problem, you will be on time for only one out of every three interviews.

Let's consider why this is so critical:

If you arrive too early

Arriving early is not the same as arriving on time. Students of motivational and sales seminars are indoctrinated with the idea that being early is somehow better. I can see the point if it's "open seating" (and therefore "open season") at the seminar, but otherwise, this is a serious mistake. When it comes to interviewing, only fools rush in.

Those time-conscious, important individuals who do enter

through the personnel department don't sit around in employment lobbies filling out applications. Instead, they arrive outside the building approximately a half-hour early and survey the premises to get their bearings. They review their notes, initiate conversations, read bulletin boards for information, and are friendly to those they meet. They may eat a light snack and perhaps drink a cup or two of coffee.

Incidentally, I recommend coffee highly as insurance to keep you on your toes during the interview and improve your attentiveness and attitude. Coffee has a predictable, harmless, positive effect for interviewing purposes. Caffeine is more than just a stimulant—it is an anti-depressant and actually has been proven to cause the neurons in the brain cells to fire faster. This means you actually will store and retrieve information more rapidly. That is why many organizations provide it to employees without charge.

If coffee makes you jumpy and irritable, or if you have a history of digestive or blood pressure problems, try regular tea instead. It's less powerful, but has fewer side effects.

Eating a light snack is mentioned not only to avoid an attack of the "munchies," but also because you don't want your blood sugar level to drop abruptly. This can make you irritable, and prone to fatigue. The best snacks are those convenient packages of cracker sandwiches with cheese or peanut butter, since the proportions of starch, protein, and bulk are just right. The worst snacks are fruit and candy, since they will accelerate the drop in your blood sugar level.

Back to our early birds: They find the restroom and "rest," they check themselves out in the mirror, freshen up; and, promptly, eyes forward, chin up, shoulders back, stomach in, feet straight, confidently, self-assured, poised, in they march, over to the receptionist, introduce themselves politely and state whom they are there to see. Then they give the receptionist the neatly typed application he so thoughtfully mailed a few days before.

I know you were thinking about all of these things anyway, so here's the even more important reason not to arrive too early: It pressures the interviewer. Interviewers don't like to be pressured any more than they are. They have ways of dealing with you.

If your appointment is with an executive or supervisor, use the same technique, although an application may not be necessary.

If you arrive too late

Arriving too late demonstrates that you are not time-conscious. It also demonstrates that you are not considerate.

Yes, interviewers are human, and will understand if you telephone ahead to offer rescheduling the appointment because there is unforeseen traffic congestion (winning applicants are never lost), a hold-up in progress, or any of your other garden-variety excuses. However, if you do not think fast, you will be subject to the following unwritten rule, which I have just written: INTERVIEWERS WHO WAIT DON'T SCREAM, THEY SCREEN.

As I said, they have ways of dealing with you. Leave as unceremoniously as you arrived, wait six months, and start reading at Chapter I.

The more important reason to avoid being late is that it will be necessary for you to start out the interview with an apology. This directly feeds into the subordinate role of an applicant and automatically turns your first serve into a fault. Do your apologizing, if at all, by telephone, before you set foot at the base line.

5. THE MAGIC FOUR HELLO.

The initial greeting with the interviewer is particularly critical, since this is when the stereotype seeds are planted. Professional interviewers unconsciously form rigid first impressions owing to the large volume of contacts they make, the "fire-fighting" nature of their duties, and the arbitrary and inconsistent requirements imposed by law and management. Stereotyping, like insisting on resumes, becomes a matter of survival.

If this seems an overstatement, consider that in companies with under 500 employees, it is not unusual for wage and salary, insurance, employee benefits, labor relations, affirmative action, management development, security, medical, training, safety, mail, telephone operations, plant maintenance, food service, company functions, civic activities, and a variety of other administrative duties to be performed by the same person who just walked out to talk to you about the same position everyone else in the lobby is applying for. Expediency and stereotyping are the order of the day, and the greeting may be your first and only chance before the interruptions start.

The Magic Four Hello consists of the following simultaneous acts:

1. A smile.
2. Direct eye contact.
3. The words, "Hi, I'm (first name) (last name). It's a pleasure meeting you."
4. A firm but gentle handshake.

As before, practice makes perfect in coordinating these four elements. Aside from making the Magic Four flow naturally, a proper handshake is often the hardest to master.

Enthusiasm in the handshake properly sets the tempo of the interview. However, the law of averages we discussed with regard to arriving on time also applies here: Experienced interviewers know that they will be subjected to "bone crusher" handshakes approximately one-third of the time. Another third will be "dead fish" handshakes. One type is painful, the other is cold, but both create a negative impression. If you have either of these problems, I would recommend that you practice shaking hands with your friends. They may get tired of you, but your career may depend on it.

Down the shelf from *Power!* and *Dress for Success* is a book entitled *Contact: The First Four Minutes,* by Leonard Zunin. It emphasizes the importance of first impressions and contains an entire chapter on the importance of the handshake.

> A moist palm may merely show someone is nervous, a symbol which automatically eliminates any job applicant at at least one large company of which I am aware. Its personnel director once told me that regardless of the qualifications of a man he interviews, "if his handshake is weak and clammy, he's out." Such reaction to body language is probably far more prevalent than we realize, as others assume many things about our glance, stance, or advance.
>
> We shake hands thousands of times in a lifetime, and it is unfortunate that most of us get little or no feedback on whether or not others like or dislike our handshake.[4]

Dr. Zunin actually conducts handshake workshops. The participants receive ratings from others far different from their own. Make sure yours is above average.

6. AVOID ASSUMING A SUBORDINATE ROLE.

If you could videotape your way through the maze you followed after the Magic Four Hello, you would find at least a hundred different cues that could influence the outcome of the interview. Examples are the color scheme, the temperature, the pictures on the walls, a glance at the employees, and an overheard remark.

Even the liveliest child is quiet in a new environment. Fear and dependence upon factors beyond your control, coupled with being under close scrutiny, can cause you to play a subordinate role.

Some applicants are aware of this danger and overcompensate by attempting to write the script for the interview in advance. This gives them a plastic, unnatural image which gets them nothing except more dress rehearsals.

The "instant replay" effect of unsuccessful interviews is

psychologically devastating and turns them into self-fulfilling prophecies for the future. In *Psycho-Cybernetics,* Dr. Maltz recalls how a similar problem affected one of his patients.

> His fear and nervousness were overcome in just one counseling session, during which I asked him: ... "Would you go into a man's office with your hand out like a beggar and beg for a dime for a cup of coffee?"
>
> "Certainly not."
>
> "Can't you see that you are doing essentially the same thing, when you go in overly concerned with whether or not he will approve of you?"

Thank you, Dr. Maltz! And thank you also for:

> Many of us unconsciously and unwittingly, by holding negative attitudes and habitually picturing failure to ourselves in our imagination, set up goals of failure.[5]

It all comes down to the basic human needs for security, safety, and acceptance. The more you analyze them, the more complicated they become.

Fortunately, there is a simple, fail-safe device that you can use to avoid assuming a subordinate role: COMPLIMENT THE INTERVIEWER ON SOMETHING IN HIS OFFICE, AND ASK ADMIRINGLY ABOUT IT. Then plan to do a lot of listening. You will notice a statuette of a hula dancer from Maui, or some equally interesting artifact. The more the interviewer talks, the more you are learning. And not about Maui, either.

7. ALIGN WITH THE INTERVIEWER.

WILL ROGERS: I never met a man I didn't like.

JEFF ALLEN: Neither did I. That's why I never saw a job I couldn't get.

If you ask around, you will find that many people have found they have the intuitive ability to obtain any job they want. This is because somewhere along the line they discovered that *liking the interviewer* dramatically invokes a powerful law of human motivation: PEOPLE LIKE PEOPLE WHO LIKE THEM.

A job interview is not the place to demonstrate your fierce and rugged individuality. In *Power!*, Korda concludes a chapter entitled "Nice Guys Finish First" by stating:

> A great deal can be gained by simply learning to smile, an exercise which is not all that easy for many people to perform. The person who wants to use power must learn to control his facial muscles, his temper and himself, and avoid taking "tough stands" where they aren't necessary. Flexibility and cheerfulness are better weapons than brute force, and if used properly have the advantage of making your rivals forget that you're a competitor for power.[6]

During my first day on the job as an employment interviewer, I was warned to avoid the "halo effect." Seventeen years later, I am still no closer to explaining how this can be done. The halo effect simply means that when you identify with an applicant, he can do no wrong. It is a psychological fact which, if you know how to make it work for you, can zap any interviewer into submission within seconds.

The formula for your ammunition is carefully secreted within the July 1979 issue of *Psychology Today*. If you want to learn its detailed ingredients, go directly to your local public library, find it, and turn to page 66. There it is: "People Who Read People," by Daniel Goleman. The ammunition is known as "pacing."

Pacing is an accepted psychological technique which has been developed to increase rapport with others. It stems from an even more powerful law of human motivation: WE LIKE PEOPLE WHO ARE LIKE OURSELVES. If you think about it, our entire hiring process is guided by this law. So is almost every other human decision we make about others, including voting, selection of spouses and friends, television and radio choices, product purchases, etc. For our highly specialized purpose, it means *aligning* yourself with the overworked and underpaid interviewer, and then leading (steering) him almost imperceptibly, but irresistibly, into extending the offer.

I use pacing all the time in court proceedings, administrative hearings, negotiations, and other difficult situations. You can win the ones you thought were lost if you know how to do it properly. I introduced the concept of pacing to placement services in my seminars about five years ago. It has been so effective in influencing hiring authorities, that many of them have incorporated the techniques you are about to learn in their standard operating procedures. It even works over the telephone and can be used during the Deep Breath Phone Call. You simply must have a common ground before you can move toward a mutual goal.

How are you going to do it? Here we go:

A. Learn job-related employment and company buzz words.

Buzz words are the "insider" language that has developed in every subculture since Adam talked to Eve. Their primary use in pacing is to lock in the alignment with the interviewer. Once you are inside his head, you can lead him effectively. Their use also gives the impression of a working knowledge of how the system works and makes you look professional. These two attributes make them an indispensable part of a successful interviewing strategy.

If you are already working in the field, you should be able to use job-related buzz word fluently. Every occupation has them, and you should know what they are. Company buzz words can be learned by using the two methods described earlier for familiarizing yourself with the employer. The following list is all you will need for employment buzz words and definitions:

Acceptance. The easiest response to any job offer. "When do I start?" are the words used.

Available labor pool. What you are walking on, rather than swimming in.

Contact information. Your name, address, and telephone number(s).

Curriculum vitae. The resume of a nuclear physicist.

Exit interview. The termination debriefing when you should say nice things about your former boss and everyone else.

Fired. Something you should avoid being. If it occurs, discuss a possible resignation with the firing authority.

Internal referral. Someone working for your potential employer who will act as your public relations representative.

Involuntary termination. One of two ways employment is severed. Generally refers to layoffs and termination for cause. The latter is the same as being fired, and requires the same corrective action.

Job comparability. The similarity between what you have done and what the employer is considering for you to do. Even if they appear totally different, 90 percent or more of every job is comparable. It's all in the eye of the beholder.

Job congruence. The extent to which the job being offered conforms to what you want to do. Your attitude should be that they are identical, or congruent.

Job description. An internal list of the duties of a particular position. Looks good on paper, but tells you more about the individual who wrote it than the job.

Job order. Authorization to a placement service containing a summary of the position, salary range, and type of individual sought. Generally bears no similarity to the person eventually hired.

Job rotation. A system whereby some employers designate certain employees to rotate jobs, so each learns the functions of a certain activity.

Labor grade. A device used in wage and salary administration to rank jobs in order of their value and compensation.

New start ("new hire"). What you will be on your first day at Company X.

Offer. Something you receive as a result of packaging and selling yourself properly. Often occurs at the time of the first interview after following the techniques in *How to Turn an Interview into a Job.*

Opportunity. The employer has a great one for you.

Qualifications. Combination of "*quality*," "*fit*," and "*occupation.*" You have them.

Personal references. Those dependent on you for support or who owe you money.

Professional references. Former instructors, supervisors, coworkers, and other people familiar with your academic or occupational history and qualifications.

Rate range. A device used in wage and salary administration to determine the lowest and highest amount that will be paid for a specific job. A critical consideration for incumbents in any position.

Resume. Something with your contact information, room for notes, job history, and enough class to generate an appointment for an interview.

Requisition ("rec"). The form that is initiated by a supervisor to obtain approval for hiring. Once the approval cycle is completed, it becomes an open requisition ("open rec").

Span of control. The number of subordinates a supervisor can handle effectively. Varies widely depending upon the capability of the supervisor, type of subordinates, complexity of the jobs, physical proximity, and amount of empire building permitted.

Voluntary termination. One of two ways employment is severed. Generally refers to leaving for a better position.

B. Develop your "action vocabulary."

The following seventy-two words should become part of your speech during the interview. They are the words of the winners in life, and they have the uncanny effect of investing you with their vitality.

While you can just photocopy the list and glance at it regularly, the best way to weave these words into your vocabulary is to write ten of them on your old business cards (or cut up some index cards), and place the cards in your wallet or purse. Take them out frequently during the first week and make up positive sentences about yourself, using one word per sentence. The following weekend, do the same with another ten words. Repeat this process until you have completed the entire list. You will be amazed at the improvement in your speech and your attitude. Most importantly, you will probably be hired long before this exercise is through.

Of course, there are other words, but these are the "heavies":

Ability	Energetic	Precise
Accelerate	Enthusiastic	Pride
Accurate	Establish	Produce
Active	Evaluate	Professional
Affect	Excel	Proficiency
Aggressive	Excellence	Provide
Analyze	Expand	Recommend
Attitude	Expedite	Reliable
Capable	Focus	Responsible
Careful	Generate	Results
Common sense	Guide	Simplify
Conceive	Implement	Skill
Conduct	Improve	Solve
Conscientious	Incisive	Streamline
Control	Initiate	Strengthen
Develop	Innovate	Success
Diplomatic	Lead	Systematic
Direct	Listen	Tactful
Discipline	Monitor	Thorough
Drive	Motivate	Train
Dynamic	Participate	Trim
Effective	Perform	Urgency
Efficiency	Persuade	Vital
Eliminate	Potential	Win

These are great to wake up a tired resume and follow-up letter as well.

C. Internalize a few success phrases.

In his popular book *The Psychology of Winning*, Denis Waitley states:

> Perhaps the most important key to the permanent enhancement of self-esteem is the practice of positive self-talk. Every waking moment we must feed our subconscious self-images, positive thoughts about ourselves and our performances ... so relentlessly and vividly that our self-images are in time modified to conform to the new, higher standards.

> Current research on the effect of words and images on the functions of the body offers amazing evidence of the power that words, spoken at random, can have on body functions monitored on bio-feedback equipment ... that's why Winners rarely "put themselves down" in actions or words.[7]

You've just learned the winner's vocabulary. Success phrases are the winner's motivation. Here are some of my favorites:

> *You never fail, you just give up.*
> *Work is not only the way to make a living, it's the way to make a life.*
> *The people who succeed are the people who look for the opportunities they want; and if they don't find them, they make them.*
> *We must be self-made, or never made.*
> *We become not only what we think, but what we do.*
> *As long as you stand in your own way, everything seems to be in your way.*
> *Procrastination is a roadblock in the path of success.*
> *When you try hard, you are almost there.*
> *We become not what we think, but what we do.*

The hardest work in life is resisting laziness.
A glimpse of an opportunity is an opportunity wasted.
The best investment you can make is in yourself.

Initially, the suggestion of internalizing success phrases may appear abstract and unimportant. Perhaps you'll discover other quotes (try *Bartlett's Familiar Quotations*) that mean even more to you. Or maybe you'll want to invent some yourself. But use them and you'll feel your self-confidence bloom. Tell some to yourself in the mirror at home. Rehearse a few in your mind while you're having coffee before your interview. Find the right time during the interview to slip one in, and the interviewer will sit up and take notice. Success is catching!

D. Attempt to sit next to the interviewer.

You still might end up across the desk, but at least try, even if you have to come around it to "look at this together." The reason is that you will be invoking a classic management principle: "*You* and *me* against the problem," instead of "*you* against *me*." If a couch is in the office, stand there until you are asked to be seated, since that would be the best place for your interview. Occasionally, the opportunity presents itself to have the interviewer sit on your favored side (i.e., your right side if you are right-handed). Don't fight it. Your power position is greatly enhanced.

E. Subtly pick up the interviewer's body language, facial expressions, eye movement, rate of speech, tone of voice, and rate of breathing.

You use this technique all the time with people you meet. However, the results of conscious practice will amaze and amuse you. Subtle imitating, or "mirroring," is a way to establish rapport. But beware of the impulse to literal imitation or you will destroy your effectiveness. This technique is designed only to *align, not to offend.* As you become accustomed to it, imitation will be nothing more than physical agreement.

F. Present your resume only if asked.

You want to appear organized, but it has already served its purpose.

G. Find an area of agreement, and start to lead very slowly toward the offer.

Leaning forward slightly in your seat at this phase is very effective. Typical statements you should use are:

"My background fits this position well."
"We have a good match here."
"This looks like a long-term situation."
"I'm excited about the position."
"Everything looks good."

These statements close in on the interviewer without him realizing it. The next move is his.

You're starting to turn the tide.

8. SAY POSITIVE THINGS ABOUT YOUR PRESENT (OR LAST) EMPLOYER.

I know it won't be easy. It never is! Let's face it, human beings were simply not made to work for each other. There is an enormous amount of latent hostility in the employment relationship, even under the best circumstances. Anyone who has conducted exit interviews can attest to that.

Almost every motivational and self-help authority has recognized that there is a difference between the words used by winners and losers. We have utilized this with the buzz words, action vocabulary, and success phrases.

Another reason to rehearse a positive statement is that the interviewer may interpret your negative comments as revealing inappropriate information about your present (or last) employer. You risk the possibility that he will anticipate the same treatment, in the event you are hired. The final reason for rehearsing a positive statement is that your leather lunch box is not the only baggage you're bringing into the interview. Your image is closely connected with your background, and even if your former employer was a loser, accentuate the positive.

There is a definite tendency to justify your reason for being in the office by blaming your present (or last) employer. Recognizing this, you will be able to transcend this Catch-22 situation, unlike other applicants, and can actually affirmatively turn it around to enhance your image! Enter Dr. Waitley:

> Winners focus on past successes and forget past failures. They use errors and mistakes as a way to learning—they dismiss them from their minds.
>
> ... Winners know it doesn't matter how many times they have failed in the past. What matters is their successes which should be remembered, reinforced, and dwelt upon.[8]

9. ADMIRE THE ACHIEVEMENTS OF THE EMPLOYER.

Surely I don't need to convince you that flattery will still get you everywhere. People appreciate honest and sincere praise.

It is perfectly natural for you to use the information you acquired through your research and listening to mention the successes of the employer, as evidenced by the number of employees, business locations, products, sales, profits, future plans, and a variety of other elements.

Mention that the anticipated expansion of the organization will create new opportunities. State that multiple locations mean a chance to combine the resources of various facilities and bring continuity to overall corporate operations. Its products must be liked by others, or they wouldn't be in business; find out why and note it. The sales and profits are impressive if they're up, and if they're down, it's because they need more conscientious people like you. Future plans are exciting challenges, and you're ready for them.

These are the ways to tie the employer to you. No "canned" sales pitch is necessary. Go natural!

10. BE EXTREMELY OBSERVANT.

At this point, approximately 80 percent of the interview is over. Most of your anxiety is gone, and you may be getting bored. Your central nervous system will be stabilizing, and therefore may reduce your metabolic rate below normal. This is unfortunate, since the halo effect must be maintained. After all, we want more than just an acquaintance . . . we want a *friend*!

You should be using your antennae at this stage: you are looking and listening . . . receiving data for processing in the follow-up letter. Names, titles, buzz words, products, and other input.

A successful interview requires extraordinary attentiveness, and that earlier drink of coffee or tea should be working for you right about now.

Sometimes people have the urge to assess the interviewer's state of mind during the interview. My technique, developed in litigation, is the "smile count." I mentally note the number of times a judge smiles at me and subtract the number of times opposing counsel obtains this acknowledgement. It works. In addition, I have perfected my smile and a number of excellent anecdotes while keeping score. Proper use of good-natured humor breaks the barriers down so you can move in.

11. PROJECT AN IMAGE WITH STAYING POWER.

Of course, we have been discussing a positive image since the resume roulette wheel started spinning in Chapter I. However, we are now in the final stages of the interview and you will soon be gone. Studies consistently show that within an hour after your departure, up to *85 percent* of your words will be forgotten. The only tangible things left from your encounter will be the documents you submitted and perhaps a few notes.

Therefore, the best way to approach this final phase of the interview is to determine what to pack into that 15 percent. You want to be identified as possessing four major attributes:

> Enthusiasm
> Confidence
> Energy
> Dependability

If you are penetrating with direct hits regarding these personality traits, you will be far ahead of the applicant who just arrived for the next interview.

In addition, there are four subsidiary attributes that should be stressed when interviewing for any position:

> Loyalty
> Honesty
> Pride in work
> Service for value received

In professional, management, administrative, and clerical positions, you can add the last four:

> Efficiency
> Procedures
> Economy
> Profit

12. THE MAGIC FOUR GOODBYE.

The Magic Four Goodbye is exactly the same as the Magic Four Hello, with the exception of the third item.

1. A smile.
2. Direct eye contact.

3. The words, "It sounds like a great opportunity . . . I look forward to hearing from you."
4. A firm but gentle handshake.

In practicing the irresistible interview technique, there are ten things that you absolutely should not do. They are:

1. DON'T WAIT OVER THIRTY MINUTES FOR THE INTERVIEWER.

This is too long and you will be angry. You will also be coming down from the psychomotor peak which occurred from the anticipation a half hour before. Politely tell the receptionist you cannot wait more than fifteen minutes longer. Make sure she notifies the interviewer immediately.

If you go through with the interview anyway, do it for practice only, because that is all you will probably get.

2. DON'T WEAR A COAT, HAT, OR OTHER OUTDOOR CLOTHING.

Remove any outer garments in the reception area. Wearing them psychologically separates you from the interviewer, makes you appear to be a stranger, and gives the impression that you were late or want to leave. All of these vibes and others are negative. If possible, also avoid taking them with you into the inner office. It is awkward and distracting.

3. DON'T WEAR SUNGLASSES.

You will be eliminating one of your most important devices: direct eye contact. This, and your impersonal look, will insure that you will not be hired.

4. DON'T ADDRESS THE INTERVIEWER BY HIS FIRST NAME.

It should always be either "Mr." or "Ms." unless you are asked to be more familiar. If he calls you by your first name, ask whether he minds if you reciprocate.

5. DON'T SMOKE OR CHEW GUM.

Asking for permission is the same as apologizing. Even if the interviewer consents, smoke is the last thing you want in the office. Smokers don't realize the offensive odor tobacco leaves on their breath, hair, hands, and clothes. They are also higher health risks, raising sick leave, disability, and group medical insurance payments dramatically. Therefore, even if the interviewer smokes, you shouldn't.

Since this is no time to quit, buy one of the over-the-counter nonsmoking tablets. Read the label, and choose one that has no warnings about blood pressure, heart conditions, or drowsiness. Those that do generally contain either stimulants or sedatives that can affect your reactions. Try out the tablets a few days before the interview so you will be able to judge if there is any difference.

As for chewing gum, don't. It just looks tacky.

6. DON'T INTERRUPT THE INTERVIEWER.

If you find yourself doing so, you should recognize that you are out of sync. Bring yourself back down to the pacing level.

7. DON'T OBJECT TO DISCRIMINATORY QUESTIONS.

Answer them as good-naturedly as you can. Don't even mention that you know they are illegal. This is no time to display your knowledge or your anger.

8. DON'T LOOK AT YOUR WATCH DURING THE INTERVIEW.

This, and other indications you are anxious, will pressure the interviewer and interfere with the rapport that should be developing.

9. DON'T READ ANY DOCUMENTS ON THE INTERVIEWER'S DESK.

This is not only bad manners, it is meddling in something which is not your concern. Even if the information is interesting, avoid the temptation.

10. DON'T PICK UP ANY OBJECTS IN THE INTERVIEWER'S OFFICE.

Many people closely identify with the objects in their office, and psychologically they may actually feel they are extensions of themselves. Even if nothing is said, this is never appreciated, and causes some interviewers to terminate the interview early, without comment. And you know what *that* means!

The Interrogation Interview: Hope It Happens

Technological advances and economic chaos have occupationally displaced record numbers of Americans. This has resulted in a virtually permanent "buyer's market," with the prospect of full employment nothing more than a dream of the past. In this environment, the "interrogation interview" is common. Interrogation interviews always contain a number of offensive questions designed to place you on the defensive.

Sometimes, this is an attempt to test your ability to react to stress. (In fact, it is also known as a "stress interview.") Other times, it is nothing but another defense mechanism . . . the interviewer's response to stress. (Similarly, the "send me a resume" and "fill out an application" routines may simply be an expression of an interviewer's own exhaustion that day.)

At its worst, the interrogation interview may have a physical setting right out of a police scenario: a smoke-filled room, inadequate lighting, improper air conditioning, uncomfortable temperature, and, of course, a hard-back chair that squeaks. More subtle interviewers create the same effect simply by sitting in front of a bright window so that the glare puts you at a disadvantage.

That's the "Interrogation Interview" half of the title. The "Hope It Happens" part arises because you will *absolutely shine!* Effectively, you will be so far ahead of the competition that your bloodshot eyes will be filled with tears of joy as you arrange for the preemployment physical.

The trick is so simple, it's amazing that other people don't use it. Scores of people through the years have taken my advice and have virtually brought interrogation interviewers to their knees. I can picture an interviewer with his chin stretched over his desk, begging some candidate to accept the offer he's extending for the position.

Gaining confidence in this situation is just a matter of practicing answering difficult questions in front of a mirror, with a tape recorder running. The typical interrogatories below are some, but certainly not all, the questions you may be asked. The answers demonstrate the technique, but must be honest for you. If you decide to rehearse your own answers, be sure that you come out of each one neutralizing the sting of the question. Of course you should adapt the actual wording to your own way of speaking.

Remember, you want to sound as though you were thinking of the question yourself. Answer in a sincere, direct manner, and move through the volley as quickly as courtesy will allow, so you can transform the interrogation interview into the irresistible interview.

The questions and answers are as follows:

1. WHY ARE YOU LEAVING YOUR PRESENT POSITION?

A. I'm interested in additional responsibility and learning more about the area of _____. The opportunity in my present position is limited because of the: (a) size of the company, (b) limited product line, (c) emphasis of the company on other areas.

2. HOW FAR DO YOU THINK YOU CAN GO IN COMPANY X? WHY?

A. Eventually, I'd like to work my way up to being _____. Of course, this will depend upon a number of factors. I think the environment in Company X is conducive to the development of its employees. Your _____, _____, and _____ are all excellent. I'm interested in contributing to its goals and know my efforts will be recognized.

3. WHAT ARE YOU LOOKING FOR IN A JOB?

A. I've found that as with almost anything else, you get out of something what you put into it. I also know that every job has its challenges. Therefore, the position of _____ should provide the opportunity I'm seeking.

4. WHAT ARE YOUR CAREER OBJECTIVES?

A. I'm looking for a company where I can contribute to its goals. Company X has a reputation for rewards commensurate with your performance. Therefore, my career objectives are to work my way into a _____ position. I want to learn as much as I can, so that as opportunities for advancement arise, I'll be ready.

5. WHY SHOULD WE HIRE YOU?

A. I've talked with a number of your employees and know Company X by reputation. It appears to be a good match and would probably result in a long-term relationship.

6. WHAT CAN YOU DO FOR US THAT SOMEONE ELSE CANNOT DO?

A. My references are the best people to answer this question. However, I think they would agree that I believe in doing my best at whatever I do. Not everyone I've worked with does this.

7. DO YOU LIKE TO WORK? WHY?

A. Yes. There is a saying, "Work is not only the way to make a living, it's the way to make a life." It's true. I'm a work-oriented   person,   and   really   enjoy   being   a

_____.

8. WHAT KIND OF SALARY ARE YOU WORTH?

A. This should be relative to my contribution to Company X. While I expect an increase to make a move, I know you will be fair.

9. WHAT WERE YOUR FIVE BIGGEST ACCOMPLISHMENTS IN YOUR LAST JOB?

A. _____
_____
_____
_____
_____

10. WHAT WERE YOUR FIVE BIGGEST ACCOMPLISHMENTS IN YOUR CAREER?

A. _____
_____
_____
_____
_____

11. CAN YOU WORK UNDER PRESSURE, DEADLINES, ETC.?

A. I've been particularly successful at working under pressure. For example, in my last position _____. You're in a competitive business, and deadlines are a way of life.

12. WHAT KINDS OF PEOPLE DO YOU LIKE?

A. I like people I can trust. My friends are from all walks of life, but they have two things in common: dependability and personal integrity. I'm very fortunate.

13. WHAT KINDS OF PEOPLE DO YOU DISLIKE?

A. People who say one thing and do another. Differences of opinion will occur, but honestly discussing them with the other person can go a long way toward resolving them.

14. WHY DIDN'T YOU DO BETTER IN SCHOOL?

A. I guess I was involved with other activities and growing up. I always got along with my teachers and classmates. I even won a _____, _____, and was recognized by _____.

15. WHY DID YOU CHANGE JOBS SO FREQUENTLY?

A. I really didn't plan it that way. At _____, it was a matter of no opportunity for advancement. My supervisor was an excellent teacher, and delegated duties to me regularly. I simply outgrew the position. When I was at _____, the company was purchased by _____, and the facility was closed. I then went to _____, and planned to grow with the company. However, when _____ learned about my background, they recruited me away with a 20 percent increase and exciting long-range plans for the company and myself. Unfortunately, the market for _____ has changed and my career could not develop further there.

16. WHAT IS YOUR BIGGEST STRENGTH?

A. I think my ability to get the job done is my biggest strength. I take great pride in accomplishing something efficiently, on time, and with no errors. I'm also a "team worker" and able to get along with people at different levels.

17. WHAT IS YOUR BIGGEST WEAKNESS?

A. Sometimes my _____ tells me I'm too concerned about doing a good job at work. I suppose that could be viewed as a strength also, though.

18. WHAT MAKES YOU ANGRY?

A. I don't get angry at other people very often, and am considered very patient by those who know me. If I had to find something, it would probably be someone who intentionally does not do his job properly. If you're getting paid, you owe it to your employer and the customer to do your best.

19. HOW LONG WOULD IT TAKE YOU TO MAKE A CONTRIBUTION TO OUR COMPANY?

A. I anticipate it would be almost immediately. I know what I'm doing, learn quickly, and expect a lot from myself.

20. HOW LONG WOULD YOU STAY WITH OUR COMPANY?

A. From all I've been able to find out, this should be for a long time. The personality of Company X appears to match my own, and I think the relationship would work out well.

21. ARE YOU WILLING TO TRAVEL?

A. Yes. I have a great family that understands "business is business." I'm used to traveling and have learned to adapt to living out of a suitcase.

22. ARE YOU WILLING TO RELOCATE?

If you are: A. Yes. I can't think of any region in the country that I would find really unacceptable. After all, every inner city has its suburbs. The only real differences are the weather and the accents. My family can always return to _____ to visit.

If you are not: A. Not unless the opportunity is really exceptional, since it would mean uprooting my family. However, I'd like to keep my options open. If the potential is there, I'll consider it seriously.

23. WHAT POSITION DO YOU EXPECT TO HAVE IN FIVE YEARS?

A. This depends not only upon my work performance, but also on the growth of Company X. However, I hope to be in a position of responsibility in the _____ area.

24. WHAT DO YOU THINK OF YOUR PREVIOUS BOSS?

A. I like my supervisor, and like the opportunity he gave me to be productive. My reasons for leaving relate more to the circumstances of not being able to use my potential.

25. WHY HAVEN'T YOU OBTAINED A JOB SO FAR?

A. I've received a number of offers. However, an opportunity like this one has not been available.

**26. WHAT FEATURES OF YOUR PREVIOUS JOBS
HAVE YOU LIKED?**

A. _____

_____

_____

**27. WHAT FEATURES OF YOUR PREVIOUS JOBS
HAVE YOU DISLIKED?**

A. _____

_____

_____

**28. WOULD YOU DESCRIBE A FEW SITUATIONS IN
WHICH YOUR WORK WAS CRITICIZED?**

A. I really can't recall any major criticisms. If anything,
I've been complimented on it regularly ... Oh, yes, once
someone made a comment about _____, but
_____.

29. WHAT WAS THE LAST BOOK YOU READ?

A. (If you're not an avid nonfiction reader, read a popular
how-to to discuss.)

30. WHAT WAS THE LAST MOVIE YOU SAW?

A. (If you're not a regular moviegoer, mention a popular
noncontroversial movie on television.)

**31. WHAT INTERESTS YOU MOST ABOUT THIS
POSITION?**

A. The opportunity it presents for someone to
_____.

32. WHAT INTERESTS YOU LEAST ABOUT THIS POSITION?

A. I don't really see any major negative aspects.

33. DON'T YOU FEEL YOU MIGHT BE BETTER OFF IN A DIFFERENT TYPE OF COMPANY?

A. I've evaluated Company X fully. The overall environment and the position you are offering make it particularly attractive.

34. WHY AREN'T YOU EARNING MORE MONEY?

A. I suppose everybody wants to earn more money. However, job satisfaction and long-range opportunity are important, too.

35. WILL YOU BE OUT TO TAKE YOUR BOSS'S JOB?

A. No. However, I think it's my job to help my supervisor advance with Company X. I should also be learning so I can eventually step into his shoes. To that extent, I suppose I am after his job.

36. ARE YOU CREATIVE? GIVE AN EXAMPLE.

A. Yes. There's almost no job that can't be done better. For example, in my last position, I _____.

37. ARE YOU ANALYTICAL? GIVE AN EXAMPLE.

A. Yes. Being able to analyze is an important part of being a good _____. For example, in my last position, I _____.

38. HOW WOULD YOU DESCRIBE YOUR PERSONALITY?

A. Even-tempered. There are two sides to every question, and I've found that a lot more can be accomplished by people working together. I always try to look at things as *"you and me against the problem,"* rather than *"you against me."*

39. WHAT DO YOU LIKE TO DO IN YOUR SPARE TIME?

A. I read a lot in the _____ field. It helps me to be a better _____, and I can bring new ideas to the job. I also spend time doing _____, since I enjoy my occupation even when I'm not getting paid. Of course I really enjoy my family as well.

40. HOW IS YOUR FAMILY LIFE?

A. Excellent. My family is very supportive. This makes it all worthwhile.

41. WHAT DO YOUR SUBORDINATES THINK OF YOU?

A. They respect me and understand we have a job to do. I try to recognize them for their achievements and have trained them to take over when I'm not there. They appreciate that.

42. CAN YOU DELEGATE RESPONSIBILITY? GIVE AN EXAMPLE.

A. Yes. This is an important part of being a manager. First it's necessary to train your subordinates so they can assume the responsibility delegated. For example, in my last position, I _____.

43. HAVE YOU HIRED PEOPLE BEFORE? WHAT DO YOU LOOK FOR?

If you did: A. Yes. I look for a dedication to work and a willingness to learn. The ability to get along with others is also important, because "no man is an island."

If you did not: A. Not directly. However, I was asked my opinion about applicants. I'd look for a dedication to work and a willingness to learn. The ability to get along with others is also important, because "no man is an island."

44. HAVE YOU FIRED PEOPLE BEFORE? WHAT REASONS CAUSED YOU TO DO SO?

If you did: A. Yes. Primarily for poor work performance. I tend to expect a lot, and let's face it, not everyone is dedicated to quality.

If you did not: A. Not directly. However, I was often asked my opinion on other employees' work performance. It's not easy to say something negative about a coworker, but the supervisors knew I expected a lot. Let's face it, a dedication to quality is best for everyone.

45. WHAT ARE THE TYPES OF JOBS YOU ARE CONSIDERING?

A. (Stress the elements of the job Company X is offering.)

46. WHAT OTHER COMPANIES ARE YOU CONSIDERING?

A. I'd prefer not to say, because they have expressed an interest in hiring me. They are companies a lot like Company X, however.

47. WHAT SIZE COMPANY DO YOU PREFER TO WORK FOR?

A. It really makes no difference. However, the size of Company X seems to combine the best of both worlds, because _____.

48. TELL US ALL ABOUT YOURSELF. HOW IS YOUR HEALTH?

A. I was raised in _____, and graduated from _____ in _____. I was recruited by _____, and have held progressively more responsible positions in the _____ field. My health is excellent.

49. MAY WE CONTACT YOUR PRESENT EMPLOYER?

A. Yes, after we get together. For obvious reasons, I'd appreciate that contact not be made until we've agreed. It's likely I'll receive a counteroffer and would prefer to be the first to tell them. They would appreciate that, I'm sure.

50. MAY WE CONTACT YOUR REFERENCES?

A. Yes, after mutual interest has been established. I've selected successful people who know my personal and professional qualifications well, but I don't want to impose on them. Just let me know when you need the contact information, and I'll furnish it.

Like I say . . . hope it happens.

VI The Second Time Around: Once More with Feeling

The second interview is often equated with getting the job. Statistically, this is true about 60 percent of the time. However, there are crucial differences from your first visit. If you understand them, you can increase your chances of being hired to almost a certainty.

If your first interview was the personnel department, you will often be asked to return for another meeting. This will probably be with the supervisor and others in the department that has the job opening, which personnel calls the functional department.

We'll be concerned mainly with guiding you through this obstacle course. If you already made direct contact with the supervisor, and your second interview is with the personnel department, then you've probably already won the battle. That second interview then is merely a formality. Watching someone use a rubber stamp doesn't require much training.

As used in this chapter, "supervisor" means any functional hiring authority from the chief executive officer down.

The differences are subtle. Perhaps that is why my prolific colleagues don't discuss them. Generally, you have passed through the interviewer's office and will be working on your future supervisor. This means that you *must* use every means at your disposal to understand what makes him tick.

At this point, you should have several acquaintances within the company that you can contact. If you haven't developed them, now is the time.

One ally you probably have overlooked is the interviewer himself. He has stamped you with his seal of approval, and you can help him by closing the requisition. The interviewer also knows that if he allows too many applicants to become actual candidates, the supervisor will delay making a decision. With so many seemingly qualified people, the supervisor's decision is that much more difficult.

Call the interviewer, and after expressing your appreciation, lead into the discussion with a comment something like: "From what I understand, it looks like I'll really be able to assist _____. Is there anything I should know before we meet?"

Then listen and take notes. The interviewer will be delighted to give you his impressions. Often they are extremely incisive since he has access to the personnel files. Before you conclude the conversation, ask the interviewer if he thinks the supervisor would mind a direct call. Interpret his "No, I don't," as a suggestion that you do so.

Then call the supervisor. After saying that the interviewer suggested you call him and asking if he has a few minutes, state: "I'm looking forward to meeting you (again) on _____, at _____. Before we get together, I wonder if there's anything you'd like me to bring."

The supervisor will not be able to think that fast. In the remote event he asks for something, evaluate whether it can affect your chances adversely. If so, say something like: "I'll check to see if I have it. If not, I'll bring what I can."

This is more than just an excuse to confirm the interview. It is a chance to hear where the supervisor's thinking is going with regard to hiring you. A little industrial espionage goes a long way. And you don't have far to go.

Generally, the second interview is more *directed*. It takes one of two paths.

1. WHO ARE YOU?

Here we are, back at another irresistible or interrogation interview. Except that now, you have already developed a profile of your target (with a little help from your friends). Just keep your powder dry and follow the same approach contained in Chapters IV and V. You'll blast right through.

After all, the supervisor is going to have a lot of explaining to do if you are rejected based upon subjective factors. If the interviewer hired the supervisor originally, bonding occurred and he will be in an even more powerful position to influence the outcome.

If you do not receive an offer, the *interviewer* will suffer a rejection shock seizure! It tends to abruptly straighten the backbone.

2. WHAT CAN YOU DO FOR US?

Time to dust off the old buzz words given in Chapter IV, but really concentrate on the state-of-the-art words appropriate to the job you are considering. Hit the library. Start building up your technical vocabulary, but don't use any words or phrases that you don't fully understand. All you need is a few choice phrases. This research should not require more than a couple of hours.

We're faced with more objective criteria here, and you should be able to anticipate the questions. The interview will tend to be informational rather than personal.

Since you may be introduced personally by the interviewer, the second interview may include him. It is up to you to create a "family atmosphere." Watch where you sit, and attempt to do so next to one or both of your "cousins." The interview will tend to be more familiar and unstructured because of the introduction and the fact that you are back again.

Don't be too physical, but a slightly warmer handshake

and a possible hand on the small of the back as you're walking through the hall, one time only, will work wonders. Powerful thing, touching. But *only* if used sparingly!

You just can't lose with the stuff you use!

VII Salary Requirements? "More!"

Unless this is your first job, or you are in a collective bargaining unit, you have experienced the trauma of asking for a raise. Generally, you receive one of three reactions:

1. THE "THIS IS YOUR LIFE" ROUTINE

This orchestration is usually conducted by the more intimidating boss who calls you into his office, has your personnel folder, and looks you straight in the eye. Then he starts reading from The Book, droning a recital of all your faults, problems, and mistakes.

You are Dorothy and he is the Wizard. If he only had a heart. But he doesn't, or as he would put it, "I'd love to help you but I can't."

2. THE "YOU KNOW HOW IT IS" ROUTINE

You are still called into the boss's office, where you watch him shrug his shoulders, writhe in pain about "company policy," or roll out the heavy "we're operating at a loss" artillery. It's sincerity time, but somehow the eye contact is just not there. Neither is the raise.

3. THE "SILENT TREATMENT" ROUTINE

This is designed to punish you for not waiting until the next scheduled review. The favorite technique is to ignore you by holding closed-door meetings near your work area with everyone else. Constant impersonal telephone calls about the status of different assignments is particularly effective as well. Sooner or later, you learn the "open door" only swings out. This one is the cruelest of all. Hope you escape without contracting paranoia.

These and other routines leave scars in your subconscious about your value in dollars long after the bruises heal. The programming in your mind translates asking for a higher salary into an unmentionable. "You should be ashamed, you *ingrate!*" you say to yourself. Unfortunately, too many people carry this feeling into a new situation as well.

For most people, the real gains in earnings will occur when they change jobs. It is unfortunate, but "good ol' boys" just don't get 20 percent increases and more unless they either threaten to leave, or actually do. Onward really is upward!

In order to maximize your effectiveness at negotiating with the interviewer, you should reflect upon the salary soap operas that have victimized you in the past. If necessary, write down their scripts and relive them just long enough to understand that they really had nothing to do with your performance at all . . . only the way it was *perceived.* How do I know? Here's the secret: *The better the job you did, the more you felt you were entitled to the raise, and the worse you felt when you didn't get it.*

Negotiating a salary takes a completely opposite approach from asking for a raise. This is because it is an arm's-length transaction, and you are just an unread book with a quality cover.

This was pointed out to me on the day I was admitted to practice law in California. When I shaved that morning, I noticed a familiar face in the mirror. My father, a practicing attorney of almost a half century, came out from New York to pop a few buttons on his vest. After the swearing-in ceremony, I asked Dad, "How will anyone know I'm an attorney?" He said, "They'll know, son. You won't even have to think about it. They'll know by the way you dress, the way you speak, and the way you carry yourself."

He was right. The most powerful messages are the ones you never say.

We already noted in Chapter I that you should not disclose *any* salary on your resume. You should also avoid any discussion of it during the interview. Interrogation interviewers may try to corner you, but the best answer is always that your salary should be relative to your contribution to the employer.

If you follow this advice long enough, you may actually find interviewers who *forget* to confirm the salary before extending the offer! This is not unusual, because your salary is one of the last things an interviewer is concerned about. And interviewers and supervisors can almost always stretch if they really want you.

Another reason to defer salary discussions in larger companies is to get past the employment interviewer and to the person you will be working for. This is because the personnel "mangler" is usually responsible for employment *and* wage and "slavery" administration. He has a vested interest in his *own* empire, and a love of procedures.

If you are fortunate enough to know the salary because it is in the interviewer's spiel, *don't react.* If you know through a telephone inquiry, advertisement, internal referral, placement service, or other source, acknowledge this, but again, *don't react.* Until you hear an absolute number, you are considering the options. Of course, it would be "inappropriate" to discuss other offers—downright "unprofessional," in fact. *Now,* who holds the reins?

Negotiating a salary is much like negotiating a loan: the more you look like you need it, the less likely you are to get it.

Let the two precepts of the art of negotiating work for you: *the one who does the most talking ends up giving away the store;* and *the less you sweat, the more you get.*

Contemplate ... let the interviewer negotiate ... against himself. The question of whether you should ever disclose your present salary is something that you will have to decide for yourself. Salary is easy to verify by requiring proof from you (check stubs, tax returns, etc.) or contacting your present (or last) employer. Curiously enough, the higher the position, the less likely it is that anyone will check.

If you are prepared, the answer to a question about your salary can be creative. State the amount you will receive after your next review and your chances of receiving an increase. Overtime possibilities should also not be overlooked, since the wages are significantly higher than those paid for straight time. What about probable bonuses? Consider pay in lieu of vacation, if that is available, since your new employer probably will not be allowing a vacation for a year. I am *not* recommending falsifying any information. I *am* recommending being aware of the hidden amounts that really add up. Remember, these are worth nothing if you don't include them, and 120 percent or more if you do. (The amount of the actual salary, plus the percentage of the increase you receive.)

If the interviewer starts talking about your future to sell you on a lower salary, you should understand the game that is being played. Veterans at changing jobs know that the only future even remotely predictable is written in an employment agreement.

References into Testimonials: Lovers Never Say Goodbye

"Reference checking" is really descriptive of what goes on. During the past decade, statutory and case law in the areas of equal employment, unemployment insurance, consumer disclosure, credit reporting, libel, slander, privacy, interference with contractual relations, and wrongful termination has increased geometrically. This has led most corporate attorneys to advise against furnishing any references on behalf of former employees. The result is that the majority of applicants have no professional references. Those that do are left with cautious, impersonal, passive reporters. Your ability to develop a cadre of interested, articulate, active advocates will be like opening your engine full throttle.

PERSONAL REFERENCES

As you can see from the buzz word definition of a personal reference contained in Chapter IV, the use of these references is limited. This is because of their level of sophistication and motivation to fabricate. However, the constraints upon professional references by standard operating procedures, policies, and their own fears means that you should not foreclose this option.

You should select mature office employees with a surname different from yours. Then you should obtain their consent, and explain *exactly* what you would like them to say. Give them that high-class resume of yours, a photocopy of a recent application, a list of the image factors found in Chapter IV, and the following personal reference questions to review before and during the telephone call.

We have all bought clothes we didn't like because the salesperson said they looked good. Third-party reinforcement is a powerful force, and you can drive up the credibility of these well-intentioned people dramatically by doing your homework.

Ask them to accept the telephone call or return it immediately (offering to pay any toll charges), and to notify you of the details the moment they hang up. (Remember our analysis of the ability to recall conversations in Chapter IV.) You need the feedback and you need it *fast*. At the very least, you will have presented some good character witnesses to help your case.

Personal Reference Questions

How long have you known _____?
How do you know _____?
What is your opinion of _____?
Is he easy to get along with?
Is he usually on time?
Was he absent from work very often?
Did he bring work home very often?
Did he like his last job?
What are his primary attributes?
What are his primary liabilities?

PROFESSIONAL REFERENCES

Cultivating professional (work-related) references is far more time-consuming and often involves reliving your sordid past. The rewards are great. Deep Breath Phone Call time, just as we discussed in Chapter II.

If you are like most applicants, you've burned a few bridges along the way. Passive-aggressive references can be even more destructive than those that make negative comments. The reason is that the interviewer does not have the opportunity to consider the source. Former supervisors are often called without your permission or even knowledge, and you may be walking around under a cloud and not know it.

You know if you and your former supervisor didn't exactly need to be chiseled apart. That negative excess baggage is carried around in your unconscious, requiring that you rehearse a positive statement for the interviewer as described in Chapter IV. Don't let it stay in your memory center . . . call and make your peace as soon as possible with every former supervisor you can find. Let them know you *really* need them!

Professional references should be called, courted, and remembered during the holiday season. They shared an important part of your life and can be a great source of guidance and perspective. Although the years and distance have separated us, I am still only a telephone call away from my first supervisor, and all that followed; two became dear friends . . . life is too short.

Work-related references are generally more potent than academic ones, because business wants tangible services. A bright, positive coworker can also be used effectively and will tend to identify with your needs. As with personal references, you should obtain their consent and review their "testimony." Don't let them use the old, "Don't worry, I'll just tell them a bunch of lies" routine to get you off the phone. This is a *business* matter, and you will reciprocate.

Your resume and a photocopy of a recent application (personal data is optional) should be forwarded to your references. Furnishing the image factors is important since your message should be repeated to the interviewer. The professional reference questions that follow will complete the preparation. The procedure regarding immediate response to the interviewer's telephone call and "instant replay" to you is the same.

Professional Reference Questions

How long have you known _____?
How do you know _____?
Did you hire _____?
When was he hired?
When did he leave?
Why did he leave?
What was his salary when he left?
What were his titles?
Did you work with him directly?
Was he usually on time?
Was he absent from work very often?
What were his duties?
Did his personal life ever interfere with his work?
Did he cooperate with coworkers?
Did he cooperate with supervisors?
Did he take work home very often?
What are his primary attributes?
What are his primary liabilities?
Is he eligible for rehire?
Can you confirm the information he has given?

Friends may come and go, but *enemies remain*. Don't let them remain enemies.

IX The Better Letter: Follow-Up into Follow-Through

The follow-up letter is the last step in getting hired. However, it is the single most effective postinterview technique you can use.

We mentioned the follow-up letter in conjunction with observations during the interview. At that time, you were developing the elements for this critical device. Ostensibly, follow-up letters are merely thank-you notes. The novice applicant either doesn't send them out at all, or mumbles an apology for doing so. You are not a novice, and should be just itching to put all those items to work.

All those words you said during the interview have dwindled down to one or two remarks, and your image is fading fast. The danger is that you will be grouped with other applicants. Now is the time to rekindle some of those fond old memories and restate your image.

The letter should be on high-quality personal letterhead, typed on an electric typewriter with a carbon ribbon, fully addressed with no abbreviations, and contain the middle initial and title of the interviewer. It should be sent immediately after the interview; be brief, enthusiastic, and to the point.

Reiterate your primary assets and accomplishments, and convincingly describe how you can benefit the employer. The properly spelled names of people you met and buzz words familiar to the interviewer should be included carefully, and it should end a lot like the words of the Magic Four Goodbye, requesting a reply as soon as possible.

Here are a few middle-of-the-road approaches for you to adapt, to make a bit more formal or more highly personalized, depending on your sense of the character and personality of the interviewer.

Some things always to be included:

1. ADDRESS LINE

The full company name, full address (no abbreviations), full name of the interviewer and his full title. These make you look thorough and professional.

2. SUBJECT LINE

"Re: Interview for the Position of ____(title)____ on ____(date)____."

This zeros in on the contents and dresses up the letter.

3. GREETING

"Dear Mr./Ms. (last name) ,"

"Miss" or "Mrs." should not be used unless you know the interviewer does so. First names are out of the question even if they were used during the interview.

4. OPENING

a. "It was a pleasure meeting with you last (day) to discuss the opening in (department) with Company X."

b. "I appreciated meeting with (name) and yourself

in your office on ___(day)___ to discuss the ___(title)___ position with Company X."

  c. "Thanks again for taking the time to see me regarding the opening in ___(department)___."

Again, comment on or add to something discussed during your interview in the body of the letter. Choose a topic that allows you to emphasize directly or implicitly your qualifications. This will keep your follow-up from being just another routine thank-you.

5. BODY

  a. "From our discussion, and the fine reputation of your organization, it appears that the ___(title)___ position would enable me to fully utilize my background in _____."

  b. "I was particularly impressed with the professionalism evident throughout my visit. Company X appears to have the kind of environment I have been seeking."

  c. "The atmosphere at Company X seems to strongly favor individual involvement, and I would undoubtedly be able to contribute significantly to its goals."

6. CLOSING

  a. "While I have been considering other situations, I have deferred a decision until I hear from you. Therefore, your prompt reply would be greatly appreciated."

  b. "It's an exciting opportunity, and I look forward to hearing your decision very soon."

  c. "The ___(title)___ position and Company X are exactly what I have been seeking, and I hope to hear from you within the next week."

7. SALUTATION

"Sincerely,"
"Very truly yours,"
"Best regards,"

If you do not receive a response within a week, reread Chapter II, and modify the Deep Breath Phone Call accordingly. If you have been interviewed by the decision maker rather than a personnel officer, a slightly different phone technique is used.

First, enlist the executive's secretary or assistant as your ally, not your adversary. A courteous, firm tone of voice works wonders. Don't play guessing games to get around the front desk: an executive calling an executive *always* states his name. Only nobodies have no names. And don't ask nosy questions about the boss's schedule, hoping to catch him unguarded. A good secretary simply will not tell you. In any case, if you call very early (before 9:00 A.M.) or late (after 5:00 P.M.), you can often get your man directly.

If you speak to the secretary:

SECRETARY: Good morning, Mr. (*last name*)'s office.

YOU: This is (*first name*) (*last name*) calling. May I speak to him, please?'

SECRETARY: I'm sorry, he's stepped away from his desk/on another line/in a meeting. May I take a message?

YOU: Mr. (*last name*) and I met last week regarding the (*title*) position.

SECRETARY: One minute, please.

The boss might very well have stepped away from his desk, be on another line, or in a meeting. But more than likely the secretary is checking to see if he wants to take the call or not. If not:

YOU: When would be a good time to call back? (or) I'll hold, please.

Since you have been direct and helpful, the secretary is very likely to return the courtesy. Also be polite and stubborn: you'll get the decision maker and a decision before long.

Sometimes people with a sales background are surprised that I do not recommend "asking for the sale." This is because it is too easy to sound like you are pleading when your livelihood is on the line. Instead, the pressure point is an *answer*, because you have "waited as long as you can," have "some decisions to make," etc.

In advising you on the approach to take, I have invoked the "fiddle theory" developed by Robert Ringer in his best-selling book *Winning Through Intimidation:*

> The longer a person fiddles around with something, the greater the odds that the result will be negative. . . . In the case of Nero, Rome burned; in the case of a sale, the longer it takes to get to a point of closing, the greater the odds that it will never close.
>
> As a general rule, you should assume that time is always against you when you try to make a deal—any kind of deal. There's an old saying about "striking while the iron's hot," and my experience has taught me that it certainly is a profound statement in that circumstances always seem to have a way of changing.[9]

Concentrate on a well-drafted letter as I have suggested, keep the pressure on the employer, and don't let the ball drop on your interview scheduling.

X The Experience Express Card: How to Leave Home with It

"How do you get experience if you don't have experience?"

That question is heard by more personnel consultants than any other. It is also the most tragic statement of all in the negativism that afflicts so many people seeking employment. The tragedy is that it is based upon the false premise that you don't *have* experience. In fact, *everyone* who is the same age has the same amount of experience. It's just that some people have more in certain areas than others. The correct question then is: "How do you get experience you can put on a resume or application, and use in an interview?" Now you're talking!

Most people would agree that the practice of law or medicine requires a high degree of knowledge and skill. However, a practicing lawyer or doctor spends less than 10 percent of professional time in anything that requires independent judgment. Even in these technical professions, over 90 percent is common sense and general knowledge. The less skilled the occupation, the lower the percentage of independent judgment required. That is the reason automation continues to displace millions of people every year.

The saying "He doesn't have ten years' experience, he has one year's experience ten times" is far closer to reality. All that matters is acquiring the maximum 10 percent knowledge that makes one job different from another. It is this phenomenon that causes a subordinate to fear a promotion to the boss's job. Once it occurs, the "bends" subside quickly. It is nothing more than an optical illusion; the view is always different from the outside looking in.

For you, the message is clear: Experience *is* the best teacher . . . so good that you need only a little bit. This reality applies whether you are starting your first job or your last. At least 90 percent is life experience.

Here's how you get it: Pick up the Yellow Pages, turn to the occupation you would like, and start phoning. Tell whomever answers you'd like to get some information on a particular field or occupation. The switchboard will probably route you through to somebody. More often than not, the person at the other end will want to be rid of you, but every now and then you'll get a talker or someone polite enough to hear you out. The more glamorous and competitive the job, the more likely they'll try to discourage you, especially if you're an entry-level applicant.

Typical phrases these Whiner's Club members use to close the doors to Experience Express applicants are:

> "It's the most competitive field you'll ever find."
> "The entry requirements are really tough."
> "It's a thankless job."
> "If I had to do it over, I never would have chosen it."
> "I wish someone had given me the advice I'm giving you now."

There isn't a single human endeavor on the face of this earth that doesn't have a minus for every plus. There are winners and losers in every field, and the only meaningful development in a career is from the inside out. What you do is not as important as how you do it. If you do it well, satisfaction and rewards naturally follow.

The discouraging words tell you more about those who say them than what they intend. I could give you a hundred examples from my life, but you just need to reflect on your own.

You should be polite, but persistent. You want something to do, and the chances are over 90 percent that you can do it with absolutely no additional training and less expensively than it is being done now (if at all). This is the one and only time in seeking employment that you should not be afraid to beg. Be flexible in your hours and earning requirements, but look for situations where duties will be varied.

Using this totally unprofessional approach may actually get you hired over the phone! Further, you'll probably have a number of interviews arranged before you get halfway through the alphabet in the first directory. If not, just keep on refusing to take no for an answer. Remember, *it's impossible to fall when you're on the floor!*

You should guard against the "emotional carry-over" which brings the rejection of the prior phone call into the new one. In *Psycho-Cybernetics,* Dr. Maltz discusses how emotional carry-over can be minimized.

> If you are using an adding machine, or an electronic computer, you must "clear" the machine of previous problems before undertaking a new one. Otherwise, parts of the old problem, or the old situation, "carry over" into the new situation, and give you a wrong answer.
>
> The exercise of retiring for a few moments into your quiet room in your mind can accomplish the same sort of "clearance" of your success mechanism, and for that reason, it is very helpful to practice it. . . .'
>
> If you have just talked with an irate and irritable customer, you need a change in set before talking with a second customer. Otherwise, "emotional carry-over" from the one situation will be inappropriate in dealing with the other.[10]

You will know you have been victimized by emotional carry-over when you call a potential employer and start the conversation by saying something like, "I didn't want your job anyway!" and hanging up the phone. But that's not going to happen if you bear in mind your goal, which is to get hired, not to get discouraged. Each call is different, each reaction will be different.

Any experience you can parlay is what you need to qualify for your Experience Express card.

The club motto is:

EXPERIENCE IS NOT WHAT YOU'VE DONE,
IT'S WHAT YOU DO WITH WHAT YOU'VE DONE.

Leave home with the card, and you'll return with offers . . . carte blanche!

CHAPTER

XI Analyzing Advertising: Help with the "Help Wanted"

The newspaper "help wanted" section appears to be an organized listing of jobs. The advertisements are in neat columns, alphabetically grouped, and often numbered by a code for the position. Unfortunately, this orderliness begins and ends in the basement print shop: it is a totally unpredictable, random, free-for-all.

The only thing you can really say is that the advertisers have put their money where their mouth is—they are paying for responses. Sometimes they even want them. They may get them, they may not. Nobody knows why.

There are five types of ads:

1. THE ONES THAT DON'T SAY WHAT THEY MEAN (25 PERCENT)

Confusing words are usually the sign of a confused mind. This occurs most often because the interviewer is rushing to meet the advertising deadline. The salesperson in the newspaper classified office is equally frantic, and the result reads like an eye chart.

A quarter of the classified advertisements are consistently unintelligible, except for the title (which may be inaccurate). A telephone call is particularly effective in these cases, because the interviewer may not have ascertained what he is looking for. An artful conversation can pace and lead effectively. It is like picking wallpaper: the first one you see will often be the one you choose. This is when you are most impressionable and when the image becomes fixed in your mind. For this reason, an immediate interview is imperative to lock in your image as a personification of the applicant to be hired.

"No" often means "maybe," so this approach can be frustrating. However, it may be the closest you ever come to customizing your job *and* your salary.

2. THE ONES THAT DON'T MEAN WHAT THEY SAY (35 PERCENT)

This advertisement appears most often and is difficult to identify with any accuracy. Many are intentionally misleading. Others are just looking for someone else. These are a major cause of rejection shock, but you should not be concerned if your telephone and mail punches don't connect.

Intentionally misleading ads are designed to bait and switch you into another position or identify you as someone seeking employment. These are the ones that seem to be "written for you" and, of course, are designed to draw the largest response possible. Glamor jobs in media and fashion industries are often featured, as are "lucrative" positions in management, marketing, and personnel administration.

Although there may be some ways you can spot these ads, I don't recommend that you attempt to do so. As with interviews, it is just another chance, and you owe it to yourself to take it. You don't have to take a job you don't want, so let them attempt to switch you all they like. If you don't want to foreclose 35 percent of the opportunities out there, don't be shy.

Inadvertently misleading advertisements contain latent ambiguities that were not obvious to the interviewer when the ad was placed. You probably will be screened out long before the appointment, since the interviewer's error will become painfully obvious to him rather quickly. This is a lesson most interviewers learn fast.

If your qualifications fit the hidden agenda, you may never discover the ambiguity. So be it.

3. THE ONES THAT DON'T KNOW WHAT THEY'RE SAYING (25 PERCENT)

These well-intentioned folks are the ones who take open requisitions and recite them in the advertisements. It takes a lot more than buzz words to really understand the specialized jobs in many companies. It takes an understanding of the personal characteristics necessary to perform the function.

Fully a quarter of all the ads you will see contain misstatements or omit essential duties. This is just because the interviewer didn't do his homework, or is trying to assure the powers that be that he is doing everything possible to find suitable applicants.

You can't really do much about this, but you stand an excellent chance of passing the initial interview by studying the advertisement carefully and using it as your theme. After all, you need to know only slightly more than the interviewer about the technical part of the job.

You'll eventually find that the supervisor who wrote the "rec" probably answered an ad just like it when he was hired!

4. THE ONES THAT SAY IT AND MEAN IT (15 PERCENT)

Yes, there are some straight talkers out there. But, alas, their seriousness means they have probably already gone through their application files, posted the job on the bulletin boards, offered "bounties" to other employees for referrals, researched wage and salary data, placed job orders, and have otherwise been disciplined in their target practice.

Your chances of getting hired probably will depend upon rigorous, objective criteria, but understanding the advertisement thoroughly and emphasizing those attributes will improve them. These ads appear only 15 percent of the time, but the employers are worth pursuing. They know what they're looking for.

5. THE ONES THAT DON'T ADMIT THEY SAID IT (10 PERCENT)

Ah, yes, those little cowards hiding inside newspaper reply boxes, able to eat their lunches. You know they're out there, but only one in twenty ever sends a reply. You're always sure it will be your boss.

Many writers warn of the horrors of sending in a resume ... can't expose yourself to this chance! They tell you all about those "lookie loos" who just want your resume to recycle the paper. Those who are considering relocating. Those who are looking to replace people just like you without telling them. Those who are afraid their competitors might find out their trade secrets. Those who are breaking the equal employment opportunity laws. Those who are running around with all sorts of diabolical plots to entrap unwary applicants into telephone-sales jobs.

Real bandits, but even the marginal ones are worth a resume. Just when you run out of stamps, someone will call. And it won't be your boss, either.

XII Placement Services: The Job Intelligence Network

Our office teddy bear, F. Lee, wears a tee-shirt that reads: "Personnel Consultants Know the Best Positions." F. Lee is never wrong.

If you are like most people, you have only a vague understanding of what private placement services really are. In this chapter, I hope to share my direct experience in all the functions we will discuss. I will then give you the perspective of a personnel manager, since I sat on that side of the desk for a while. Finally, I will share the observations from my daily contact with hundreds of these businesses.

If you familiarize yourself with how they work and think, and then seek their advice, you will greatly magnify your opportunities for advancement in your career.

Career advisors, guidance counselors, image consultants, resume services, and other miscellaneous enterprises are not included. Not even honorable mention, because their ability to get you hired is limited and their fees often are not.

The activities and effectiveness of outplacement consultants, job-finding clubs, job cooperatives, institutional placement services, and public placement services vary widely, making any generalizations impossible.

Placement services can be divided into three categories:

executive recruiters, employment agencies, and temporary employment services. Collectively, these form the "job intelligence network."

EXECUTIVE RECRUITERS (PROFESSIONAL/ MANAGEMENT/TECHNICAL RECRUITERS, EXECUTIVE/PROFESSIONAL/MANAGEMENT/ TECHNICAL SEARCH FIRMS, EXECUTIVE/ PROFESSIONAL/MANAGEMENT/TECHNICAL CONSULTANTS, "HEADHUNTERS," ETC.)

Executive recruiters are paid exclusively by the employer (client). Approximately five percent are employer-retained, and the rest operate on a nonexclusive, contingency fee basis. The fees are generally calculated based upon a percentage of the projected annual starting salary of the applicant (candidate). They average around $8,000.

These organizations tend to be owned by management and sales-oriented individuals from almost every industry. They thrive on the chase (identification) and kill (placement). They are quick of flight, have a positive attitude, sensitive faculties, and a keen sense of timing.

Several of the larger national recruiting organizations are owned by major corporations, and most have developed a franchise system. Virtually all the recruiters and office managers are compensated based upon the placement fees received or "cash in." Some (particularly the personnel management refugees from industry) use big words. Most know the ropes and the rules. If you use the techniques in this book when you contact them, all will want to present you for suitable openings. Then simply use the techniques to get hired.

Recruiters are successful because they know where the action is in the employment market. They know employers from the inside, where intramural politics and morale hide. They know who has exciting products on the boards, and who is about to lose key employees. They know who promotes from within and who stifles creativity. They know who pays well and who has high turnover. They know for the same reason you know about the interviewer ... they listen.

Executive recruiters tend to be clustered in major cities and can be found in Yellow Pages listings under "Executive Recruiting Consultants," "Management Consultants," "Personnel Consultants," "Employment Agencies," or variations on these headings.

EMPLOYMENT AGENCIES (EMPLOYMENT SERVICES, PERSONNEL AGENCIES, PERSONNEL SERVICES, ETC.)

During the past decade, over 80 percent of employment agencies have changed their fee policy from applicant-paid ("fee") to employer-paid ("free"). They are paid on a contingency fee basis, and the placement fees are calculated based upon a percentage of the projected monthly or annual starting salary of the applicant.

As you can see, there is a substantial overlap between employment agencies and executive recruiters as the starting salary increases. That is why the words they use and places they appear in the Yellow Pages are often the only differences.

If you are considering a position below $20,000, you should be focusing on general employment agencies. These specialize in clerical, administrative, semiskilled, and trainee (entry-level) placement. Even if they are employer-paid, you will find the counselors to be among the brightest, most positive human beings around. Their placements occur more frequently, and, therefore, they do not mind interruptions and assisting applicants (in confidence, if you wish). You might be talking to the owner of the business or with one of hundreds of employees.

The great strength of employment agencies is their "street sense" and flexibility to serve applicants and employers. Some are also engaged in temporary placement, expanding the options for both parties.

If you have been avoiding employment agencies because their reputation is less than sterling, I recommend that you take another look. Be prepared for an interview.

Employment agencies are found in almost all regions and are in the Yellow Pages listings under "Employment Agencies," "Employment-Permanent," "Personnel Agencies," or similar headings.

TEMPORARY EMPLOYMENT SERVICES

True temporary services seek registration from applicants interested in short-term or part-time employment. This is generally for clerical or semiskilled services, but can extend to technical disciplines as well. They then market their services to customers (clients) and charge a specific amount for the services performed, usually on an hourly basis. When the temporary assignments are given, they dispatch their employees, and charge based upon the time records which are submitted. The temporary service is responsible for all payroll deductions, and may offer additional benefits and bonuses for its employees.

A temporary assignment gives you an inside look at a company that classified ads can't. And if it works out, you'll get called back. You can find out about permanent jobs before they are advertised and get a head start on the competition. It's a great opportunity to make some friends within the company for that invaluable internal referral as well. Most temporary services offer a "temp to perm conversion" to customers so they can hire you directly after a certain period of time. This "try before you buy" policy is one of the best reasons to use a temporary agency, for both an employer and you.

Should you wish temporary employment, the Yellow Pages heading is generally "Temporary Personnel," "Personnel-Temporary," "Temporary Employment," "Employment-Temporary," "Engineering Services," "Computer Services," etc.

To summarize, executive recruiters open doors you thought were walls, employment agencies open doors you can't open yourself, and temporary services get you inside a company for a short look around. And for all of them, the interview is crucial.

They all know the rule: IF YOU DON'T MAKE IT HAPPEN, IT WON'T.

XIII Looking While You're Still Employed: Isn't Everybody?

Ongoing job market research is fun and gives you a low-risk, common-sense way to evaluate your present position. It also arms you with facts that can be used either to negotiate more effectively with your present employer, or to move more quickly if you must leave.

From the new employer's standpoint, you're more attractive if someone else thinks you're worth the salary. You communicate confidently because you're financially and emotionally more secure. These are important differences and can be used to turn any job into a springboard.

All you really need for your little do-it-yourself launching pad is high-quality personal letterhead stationery, an updated resume, access to an electric typewriter with a carbon ribbon, and a telephone answering device.

Let's consider how to maximize your effectiveness:

1. SCHEDULE YOUR PART-TIME JOB OF LOOKING.

Looking for a job really is a full-time job. But you can't sacrifice what you have for what you want.

It's easy to become an "interviewaholic" once you start thinking about your reasons for leaving. This can distract you from your primary task of earning a living, and alert your employer to your clandestine activities. You also must guard against *unconsciously* conveying your plans to your boss and coworkers. It can be a real roller coaster downhill, so be *extremely* careful in your scheduling, and do it after working hours unless you have complete privacy in your office. Secretaries, switchboard operators, and mailroom clerks are usually the first to notice the symptoms (cryptic phone calls, multiple "doctor visits," "Personal and Confidential" envelopes, etc.); you also may smile a lot.

Your approach to phone conversations and interviews should be that you are being paid to do a job, and it would be improper for you to take company time for personal business. Besides, you have a lot of responsibilities to your present employer, and want to be considered as effective as possible.

You get the picture: Use your integrity and stature as a basis for special treatment in employment interview scheduling. You'll get it, too. Why? Because you're just a little hard to get.

Evenings or weekends are fine.

2. MAXIMIZE YOUR PERSONAL CONTACTS.

These include former supervisors, coworkers, and friends. Their assistance should be sought in two ways:

Notifying you about opportunities. Their motivation to assist is best utilized by asking them to be your eyes and ears. They often delight in letting you know inside information or leads that they learned about through personal observation. You should *gently* let them know if they are furnishing information on jobs you don't want. Be grateful for any assistance, no matter how ridiculous, or you may lose more than a resource and a reference ... you may lose someone who really cares.

Presenting your background. Since they are your acquaintances, they will be working for you with the best intentions. Therefore, copies of your resume and other background information should be given to them. Delete anything you feel is too personal, but give them as much data as you can.

Personal contacts are a limited resource, since there are so few of them, and they are doing you a favor. Therefore, they should not be your only source for market research.

3. USE A TELEPHONE ANSWERING DEVICE FOR YOUR RESIDENCE PHONE.

Include your home phone number only on all correspondence and your resume, designated as "message number."

The resume shouldn't identify your present employer in any way. Use descriptions like "Major Manufacturing Company," "Medium-Sized Law Firm," "Newly Established Health Care Facility," etc.

If you use an answering device with remote capability, and you can do so privately in your office, return the calls the same day. Otherwise, early the next day is perfectly acceptable. The message should be recorded in your own voice, and state pleasantly:

> Hello! This is *(first name) (last name)*. I regret that I am unable to answer your call at this time. However, if you leave your name, telephone number, and a brief message at the tone, I will return your call as soon as possible. Thank you for calling!

While machines turn some people off, they are accepted, reliable, and consistent. Your communication already indicates that a message is all that will be taken, and an electronic device is far better than someone with poor phone manners. If you can afford it, buy one that is voice-activated, so you receive the entire message. Answering services can be extremely rude and more expensive over time, so they are not recommended for this purpose.

4. PURSUE ADVERTISEMENTS.

Mailing resumes is easy, and you shouldn't be afraid to answer blind box advertisements. In my entire career, I have encountered only fifty instances of an employee's resume being sent to his own company through a blind ad. I would estimate that in thirty of these, the employer either already knew the employee was running around the countryside or didn't care. In another fifteen, the discontent was nothing more than a communication blockage with the supervisor; the "forced communication" had a positive effect, and differences were resolved amicably. Four ended with the employee leaving voluntarily after a mutually acceptable transition period, and one was fired. That's a two percent chance. Why worry?

5. SELECT A CADRE OF PLACEMENT SERVICES.

In Chapter XII, the proper use of placement services was discussed in detail. They are the best source when you are employed, since they can present your qualifications in much the same way as a public relations representative does. They are discreet and have three things you don't: knowledge of the job market, contacts, and time. Working together, you can form a valuable alliance.

The only caution is that by now, you'll probably be considered an MPA (Most Placeable Applicant). If you receive this honor, they may try to "run" you. That means too many nonproductive phone calls and interviews.

Tell them. All celebrities have the same problem.

I hope you take this advice immediately, because the opportunities out there are just too hot to hold!

XIV P.S. Soon You'll Be Hearing . . .

Ever since the Industrial Revolution, those responsible for employment have been seeking a professional identity. The titles have become more formidable: labor supervisor . . . employment manager . . . personnel manager . . . director of industrial relations . . . vice president, human resources development. Buzz words have proliferated: aggregate work force, applicant flow data, impact ratio, progression sequence, skills inventory, utilization analysis. A job saved here, a promotion there—it's what makes the world go 'round.

We'll be interviewing on the moon in our blue space suits, and might as well be running around the caves in leopard skins for all the progress we've made in selecting one human being to work for another.

What does all this mean to you? Do you *really* think a change in the unemployment rate will help *you*? Will you feel differently if the cup is 89.9 percent full next month? Won't you still be one-on-one, getting down to business with some human being you've never met before?

The techniques in this book work. Not because I want them to, not because they're needed, but because they're based on trial and error, the same way Edison developed the light bulb. The explanations and theories are nice, if that's your bag, but they came later. Too much analysis leads to paralysis. Break out of those self-imposed shackles and do it!

Soon you'll be hearing those immortal words: "You're hired!"

Oh, just in case you missed something ... *GOOD LUCK!*

Bibliography ... and Why

I could have written this without quoting from any other books or from many others. However, I wanted to introduce you to some references that will develop your practical skills and perceptions as you move through your career. Several years ago, the great motivational speaker, Charles "Tremendous" Jones, told me, "You will be the same in five years as you are today except for the people you meet and the books you read." He was absolutely right.

The stockpile of self-help books continues to grow, with most of the additions nothing more than "smoke bombs." A flashy cover, a sexy title, an inflated claim, a self-proclaimed expert. You have no time for that nonsense; you should be assessing, restructuring, and developing the techniques that will supercharge your career. I have done your research for you, and, with one exception, they are all available in paperback. Far from being smoke bombs, they are unadulterated dynamite! Buy them, read them, listen to them, and save them as part of the survival kit you will need as you continue your journey along the road of life.

Initially you should read *Winning Through Intimidation*. You might note that Robert Ringer and I write in somewhat the same style and share the same philosophy. For this reason, his approach is particularly valuable to bridge from your specific task of finding the best position to maximizing the effect of doing so. He is a no-nonsense, get-down-to-business author, with the savvy and writing ability to back it up. (Another recommended book by Ringer is *Looking Out for Number One*, but read *Winning* now since we are attempting to maximize your perception when your time is limited.)

The next book that is must reading is *Power! How to Get It, How to Use It*. It is a well-researched and generally accurate book. I could have quoted its author, Michael Korda, more extensively, because so much of the hiring matrix is ruled by silent idols. Understand them, and you can use them to your advantage. (Korda has written an excellent sequel entitled *Success!*, but you can wait.)

Another book you should read is *Dress for Success* or its companion, *The Woman's Dress for Success Book*. While *Dress for Success* has sold over two million copies and its author, John Molloy, is the most respected clothing consultant in America, most people simply don't follow his advice. In my case, it was simply a matter of phasing out the less powerful items in my career wardrobe. My revenge has been on the weekends, but John's has been that I have fewer of them to spend with my family. *Dress for Success* contains basic truths, and selective reading can get you through the book in less than an hour. Underline and act upon the advice.

It is somewhat unusual for an author to recommend an article in a magazine several years old. However, "People Who Read People," by Daniel Goleman, is a valuable survey of the work in neurolinguistic programming. Unfortunately, the research upon which it is based is designed for the professional psychotherapist. Someday, a practical book on the subject probably will be written. I'll probably write it.

Moving down in the chronology of further homework, I recommend *The Psychology of Winning*, by Denis Waitley. It is the only book in the bibliography not available in paperback, but is inexpensively priced. Dr. Waitley has also produced a companion six-cassette album, but for now, save your money. *The Psychology of Winning* derives its value from the simple, eclectic, warm style of its author. It is not "must" reading, but it is suggested because it contains basic truths.

The next book I would recommend really doesn't belong inside a book sandwich. In a class by themselves are *Psycho-Cybernetics* and its late author, Maxwell Maltz. If you can beg or borrow the six-cassette album produced by Dr. Maltz in 1972, do so! (It is out of print now.) You will feel as though you are sitting on the lap of Methuselah, as he gives you the synthesis of 969 years on earth. The book has spawned an entire industry and is written in the same human style.

I have included *Contact: The First Four Minutes,* by Leonard and Natalie Zunin, since it dissects the all-important first impression. For interviewing purposes, the information is valuable, but at this point, you will probably find it unnecessary.

Although it has not been quoted, you might wish to review *What Color Is Your Parachute?* by Richard Bolles. It is a delightful, witty, annually updated anthology that surveys the employment field. I recommend it highly as an overview, but have found a more focused approach gets you hired.

These are the ones I recommend. May they work the wonders for you they have for countless others.

BIBLIOGRAPHY

Bolles, Richard N., *What Color Is Your Parachute?,* Berkeley, California, Ten Speed Press, 1982.

Goleman, Daniel, Ph.D., "People Who Read People," New York, *Psychology Today,* July 1979.

Korda, Michael, *Power! How to Get It, How to Use It,* New York, Ballantine Books, 1975.

Korda, Michael, *Success!,* New York, Ballantine Books, 1978.

Maltz, Maxwell, M.D., F.I.C.S., *Psycho-Cybernetics, New York, Pocket Books, 1969.*

Maltz, Maxwell, M.D., F.I.C.S., *Psycho-Cybernetics,* Scottsdale, Arizona, Tom Hopkins Champions Unlimited, 1972 (Audiocassette Series).

Molloy, John T., *Dress for Success,* New York, Warner Books, 1975.

Molloy, John T., *The Woman's Dress for Success Book,* New York, Warner Books, 1978.

Ringer, Robert J., *Looking Out for Number One,* New York, Fawcett Crest Books, 1978.

Ringer, Robert J., *Winning Through Intimidation,* New York, Fawcett Crest Books, 1973.

Waitley, Denis E., Ph.D., *The Psychology of Winning,* Chicago, Nightingale-Conant, 1979.

Waitley, Denis E., Ph.D., *The Psychology of Winning,* Chicago, Nightingale-Conant, 1978 (Audiocassette Series).

Zunin, Leonard, M.D., with Natalie Zunin, *Contact: The First Four Minutes,* New York, Ballantine Books, 1973.

Notes

1. *Power! How to Get It, How to Use It,* by Michael Korda.
2. *Psycho-Cybernetics,* by Maxwell Maltz, M.D., F.I.C.S.
3. *Dress for Success,* by John T. Molloy.
4. *Contact: The First Four Minutes,* by Leonard Zunin, M.D., with Natalie Zunin.
5. *Psycho-Cybernetics,* by Maxwell Maltz, M.D., F.I.C.S.
6. *Power! How to Get It, How to Use It,* by Michael Korda.
7. *The Psychology of Winning,* by Denis E. Waitley, Ph.D.
8. *The Psychology of Winning,* by Denis E. Waitley, Ph.D.
9. *Winning Through Intimidation,* by Robert J. Ringer.
10. *Psycho-Cybernetics,* by Maxwell Maltz, M.D., F.I.C.S.

Index

About the Author

JEFFREY G. ALLEN, J.D., C.P.C., is America's leading placement attorney. His combined experience as a certified placement counselor, personnel manager, and professional negotiator uniquely qualify him as an authority on the hiring process. Mr. Allen is Special Advisor to the American Employment Association and General Counsel to the California Association of Personnel Consultants. He writes a nationally syndicated column entitled "Placements and The Law," conducts seminars, and has often been featured in television, radio, and newspaper interviews. He lives in the Los Angeles area.